W9-DEW-517

The Joint Free Public Library
of
Morristown and Morris Township

THE LAST
SURVIVOR

THE LAST SURVIVOR

IN SEARCH OF MARTIN ZAIDENSTADT

Timothy W. Ryback

PANTHEON BOOKS NEW YORK

Copyright © 1999 by Timothy W. Ryback

All rights reserved under International and Pan-American Copyright
Conventions. Published in the United States by Pantheon Books, a
division of Random House, Inc., New York, and simultaneously in
Canada by Random House of Canada Limited, Toronto.

Pantheon Books and colophon are registered trademarks
of Random House, Inc.

Library of Congress Cataloging-in-Publication Data
Ryback, Timothy W.
The last survivor : in search of Martin Zaidenstadt /
Timothy W. Ryback.
p.   cm.
ISBN 0-679-43971-4
1. Dachau (Germany)—Social life and customs.
2. Holocaust, Jewish (1939–1945)—Germany—
Dachau—Public opinion.   3. Public opinion—
Germany—Dachau.   4. Holocaust, Jewish (1939–
1945)—Influence.   5. Jews—Germany—Dachau—
Biography.   6. Dachau (Concentration camp)
7. Holocaust survivors—Germany—Dachau—Biography.
8. Zaidenstadt, Martin.   9. Dachau (Germany)—
Ethnic relations.   I. Title.
DD901.D13R93   1999
940.53'18'094336—dc21   98-52319   CIP

Random House Web Address: www.randomhouse.com

BOOK DESIGN BY MAURA FADDEN ROSENTHAL/Mspace

Printed in the United States of America

First Edition
9   8   7   6   5   4   3   2   1

In memory
of
André Victor Luber

Since then, at an uncertain hour,
That agony returns:
And till my ghastly tale is told,
This heart within me burns.

— SAMUEL TAYLOR COLERIDGE,
"The Rime of the Ancient Mariner"

Preface

"When people see that I have made a life in the place where I was brought to die," Martin Zaidenstadt once told me as a way of explaining why he, as a Holocaust survivor, remained in Dachau, "they understand that they too must learn to forgive, that if Martin can forgive the Germans for what they tried to do to him, they can forgive as well."

It may be good advice for our blood-sotted, late-century world, and though Martin spoke these words with all the gravity and import of the last survivor offering final absolution for the worst crime ever committed by man against man, I believe this was, like much of what Martin has told me over the years, an attempt to infuse some deeper meaning into a lifetime spent in Dachau.

Though I have encountered numerous Holocaust survivors over the years, both obscure and famous, I have never met anyone quite like Martin Zaidenstadt. A Polish Jew who was shipped to Dachau by the Nazis in 1942, Martin has spent the last half-century just across town from the camp, and the last five years holding a daily vigil outside the gas-chamber door at the former concentration camp. I have presented Martin exactly as

I have experienced him. Though he has lapses of memory and judgment, I trust the reader will come to know him as I have, as a man of keen intelligence, subtle wit, and boundless goodwill.

Author's Note

All the persons in this book are actual people; however, in a few cases names and identities have been obscured for reasons of privacy. In some instances, where individuals' memories have lapsed or there have been contradictory accounts, I have taken limited artistic license in retelling their stories.

THE LAST
SURVIVOR

1

THERE IS A CLICK AS the key turns. The desk drawer
slides open. A pile of red-and-white HB cigarette packs
is knocked aside. A gun is withdrawn. As far as I can tell,
it is a standard .380 caliber pistol, not unlike the kind
that Heinrich Schmied displays in the window of his
sporting-goods shop across the street from Susan's
Café in downtown Dachau. According to Schmied,
these .380s are not very sophisticated weapons—a
seven-shot clip, recoil-operated reload, and rather limited range. An amateur sportsman can hit a target at
eight to ten meters. Anything beyond that, says
Schmied, is "a matter of luck."

But on this fine spring morning, Martin Zaidenstadt
would not need much luck. Seated opposite him at his
desk, no more than three feet away, I am an easy target.
He has just finished telling me about the execution of a
fellow inmate, Jerzy Czermanski, at the hands of the SS.
It was a beautiful spring day, not unlike this very day,
when an SS officer put a pistol to his temple and blew
his brains out. Just like this. And he points the gun in my
direction.

People in Dachau had warned me about Martin
Zaidenstadt. They said he was a tortured soul, a deeply

3

troubled man. Some said he was obsessed, others that he was deranged. Nobody told me he was armed.

Several years ago, Martin began a daily vigil in front of the camp's brick crematorium building that also houses the gas chamber. Whenever visitors approach the building, he addresses them, usually in German, though sometimes in English or Polish or Russian, and occasionally in Spanish, Yiddish, or Hebrew. I have even heard him offer passing phrases in Chinese. The man veritably speaks in tongues. None with any fluency. He speaks about things we already know—about the hunger, the cold, the fear, the myriad brutalities of camp life. He also adds fresh insights to the generic horrors. "You could always tell whether they were burning Russians or Jews," Martin recalls. "The Russians still had fat on them, and the smoke was yellow. The Jews had been starved and were nothing but skin and bones. The smoke was always blue." Or was it the other way around? Martin used to know but can't quite remember anymore. Sometimes he says that the Americans brought him to Nürnberg to testify in the 1946 trials against Nazi war criminals. "They listened to Martin," he told me, "because they knew what he told them was true."

A full-faced man with a solid constitution, Martin Zaidenstadt dresses his eighty-seven years in tweed jackets, wool pants, and sturdy walking shoes. He moves with the slow, late-life rhythm of a man who has survived many harsh decades. His weathered face seems sculpted, as if hewn from some durable stone breathed to life. Martin could be eighty-five or ninety-five or a hundred and six. It seems as though he will live forever.

But the mind is failing this solid vessel. Martin's inner compass has lost its bearing and the course of his conversation drifts and tacks with the slightest conversational breeze. Martin will pass indolently from one memory to the next, his eyes fixed on the distant shores of his youth, until he is overtaken by a squall of rage. His eyes fill with fear or anger. He fulminates and rages, and after a few moments this passes, and he again is set adrift onto other memories.

Martin holds the gun in his hand and stares at me. A gun to the temple on a clear spring morning, and a simple tug on a trigger, he has just told me. That is how people died in Dachau a half-century ago. What did I think about that?

In truth, I don't know what to think. I have had guns pulled on me before—in Detroit, in Bosnia, in Wyoming—but always by people who knew what they wanted—money, a passport, or just for me to get the hell off their land. With Martin I am not certain why he is doing this, and, more unsettling still, I am not certain he knows either. I stare into his eyes, trying to gauge his intentions. They are deep, brown, kind eyes, but now they seem fogged, clouded.

"You don't think the gun is loaded," he says, his voice suddenly challenging. I offer no answer.

Martin tilts the gun slightly to the side, presses a release, and the ammunition clip slips into the palm of his left hand, revealing nine gleaming bullets with rounded brass tips. They glint tauntingly in the morning light that pours through the window. He smiles at me, then kicks the clip back into the gun with the butt of his hand and again levels the barrel at me. I see his finger move to the trigger. Only then do I feel myself go weak.

In that instant I do not see my life flash before my eyes. Instead, I see the Zaidenstadt laundry in the backyard, an array of unbleached shirts and undergarments flapping in the morning breeze against a brilliant April sky, all the while thinking that it seems like such a waste to die on such a beautiful spring day in a suburban study at the hands of a befuddled, possibly delusionary Holocaust survivor. The gun, cushioned on a cloud of jumbled memories, drifts to the right and left in Zaidenstadt's unsteady hand, and I am trying to fathom his intentions, wondering if a quick leap to the right or left will save my life or trigger his reflexes, not certain what in the hell I should do.

We sit there face-to-face for a moment. Zaidenstadt flinches when he hears steps in the hallway. It is his wife, who has just come in the house. He drops the gun into the drawer, pushes it shut, and turns the key.

2

I FIRST CAME TO DACHAU in the winter of 1992, when Robert Gottlieb, then editor of *The New Yorker*, asked me to write a "report" on this picturesque Bavarian town fifteen miles north of Munich. Bob wanted to know how people could live in a place with a name like that, how the older people lived with the memories, how the younger people dealt with the legacy. When I asked him how long the piece should be, he asked me how long I thought it should be. When I asked him when he needed it, he asked me how long I thought it would take me to write. At the time, I had no idea, but I knew it would not be easy.

As the very epicenter of Teutonic excess and atrocity in our century, Dachau boasted the first "concentration camp," the first "crematory oven," the first "gas chamber," the first medical experiments on human beings. Dachau also served as boot camp for the tens of thousands of SS officers who were subsequently dispatched across Europe to Hitler's franchised atrocity. Rudolf Höss, the notorious Auschwitz commandant, trained in Dachau, as did Adolf Eichmann, the dark technocrat behind the Final Solution.

For all its accumulated horror, Dachau was also home to a twelve-hundred-year-old community set in the rolling hills north of Munich, a picturesque village with crossbeamed houses, cobblestone streets, and an ancient oak tree that spread vast plumes of foliage across the old market square on quiet summer afternoons. In the two months I spent researching and writing the article, I met a host of Dachau residents. Over afternoon teas and late-night dinners, they shared with me their anxieties, frustrations, and hopes. In some, I awakened long-repressed memories; in others, questions about themselves and their neighbors.

In many instances, the Dachauers asked me more questions than I asked them: the Dachau mayor, Lorenz Reitmeier, asked me why twelve years of Nazi atrocity should be permitted to negate twelve hundred years of proud history and culture? Hans Günter Richardi, a local historian, wanted to know why the Dachau residents should bear more responsibility or guilt than any other Germans, especially when voting records indicated that Dachau residents cast only 20 percent of their ballots for Hitler, compared with 40 percent for the rest of the country? "Had the rest of Germany voted the way Dachau did," Richardi told me, "Hitler never would have come to power. There never would have been a Third Reich." More than one Dachauer wanted to know why the town of Dachau had to bear this grim historical legacy when the camp was actually located in the neighboring village of Prittlbach? Why didn't I ask the Prittlbachers what it was like to live daily with the rattle of massacring SS gunfire? What it smelled like to open your window and breathe the charring flesh from the crematory ovens? To shake the human ash from your bedsheets after drying them on the clothesline? Why didn't I write a "report" on Prittlbach?

These were difficult questions, and for *The New Yorker* I provided a simple answer: I roundly condemned the residents of Dachau as small-minded and self-pitying, unwilling to accept moral responsibility for their town's role in the Holocaust. I profiled Nikolaus Lehner, a sixty-five-year-old Romanian Jew who had remained in Dachau following his liberation from the concentration camp. For a number of years, Lehner, owner of a thriving building supply company, had lobbied the mayor for the creation of a center in Dachau where young people could meet survivors and discuss issues related to the Holocaust and other atrocities. Lehner and his supporters were met with fierce resistance. One Town Council member declared that he would never allow such a center to be built in Dachau. He warned that Lehner's project would convey the impression that the entire Third Reich had taken place nowhere in Germany except Dachau; that the town would become known only as the *KZ-Stadt*, or the "concentration camp town"; that the "mark of Cain" would be pressed upon the brows of every Dachau resident for all time. Underscoring his resolve, the Town Council member declared, "We will defend ourselves with all our might, to the very last drop of blood."

High ground is, both militarily and morally speaking, the easiest to defend, and, in retrospect, I think I made an excellent choice in Lehner. His story was compact, compelling, and it allowed me to highlight the outrages and absurdities of Dachau. The article brought some well-deserved attention to Nikolaus Lehner, and confirmed for many people their worst prejudices about the Germans and their unwillingness to confront the past. As for me? I followed the exigencies of the journalistic trade. I packed away my notes, cashed my check from *The New Yorker*, and set to work on a new writing assignment.

Two months later, however, I found myself back in Dachau, this time without a writing assignment, without any clear notion of why I was there, except to contemplate many of these unanswered questions. Since then, I have come to realize that virtually every moral and political issue related to the Holocaust has played itself out in Dachau. The painful debates that occasionally cripple the German Bundestag, or entangle writers and scholars, or make headlines around the world, all have their counterparts in miniature in Dachau, at Town Council meetings or around tables in beer-sotted pubs or in the daily pages of the *Dachauer Nachrichten* and the *Dachauer Neueste*. Most of the time, however, the residents of Dachau attempt to carry on like the residents of any other town. The only difference is, they have DACHAU stamped on their birth certificates, carry DACHAU on their drivers' licenses and in their passports, pay DACHAU electric bills, DACHAU water bills, and DACHAU gas bills. I like to think of Dachau as the "Our Town" of the Holocaust era.

Like the Thornton Wilder stage piece, Dachau is a haunted place. But instead of the few narrative ghosts that spook the set of *Our Town*, Dachau is brimming with the shades of Holocaust victims. With more than thirty thousand dead buried in the surrounding hills—Germans, Jews, Russians, Poles, Frenchmen, Romanians, Hungarians, even a handful of Brits—there is virtually one extinguished life for every man, woman, and child in Dachau today. Their spirits don't just drift through town on the spring mists, or whisper through the branches of hoarfrosted trees; they rattle shop windows in broad daylight, clatter through cobblestone streets, crash town meetings, and cross the best-laid plans of mayors, shopkeepers, and real estate developers.

For years, they have whispered ever so gently to Ingrid Hauser, an attractive woman in her late fifties who had grown up in her family home directly across from the Dachau railway station. Though Ingrid retains only vague memories of that dark time, she remembers vividly the arrival of the trains. "I was six or seven, and I used to see the SS guards driving them out of the boxcars down to the camp," she told me over coffee one afternoon. "Whenever one of us asked our parents about them, they simply said 'Shhh.'" She held a finger to her pursed lips, then continued in a subdued voice: "It was not something that was talked about. It was never mentioned. Only years later did we learn about the horrible things that happened there." She paused and gazed silently through the window at the train station. It is a handsome structure with fresh sienna stucco and a black roof. There is a parking lot nearby filled with bright Mercedes-Benzes, Peugeots, and BMWs. Dachau is a prosperous community. "They would bring the prisoners in at night, I think so no one could see them. Then one thing I remember clearly is the sound of their shoes on the cobblestones. They wore shoes made of wood. I remember the clatter of all those wooden shoes against the cobblestones. It is a sound you never forget." In the silence of the Dachau night, she still awakes to the sound of wood on cobblestone.

These same shades that visit Ingrid Hauser have pursued Bruno Schachtner halfway around the globe. Born in 1938, the son of an SS officer and a local Dachau girl, Schachtner grew up just down the street from the concentration camp. His first memories are those of his father's glinting leather boots and his crisp uniform—Schachtner has a photograph of himself as a child sitting on the grass beside his father's peaked SS officer's cap—marching off to work each morning, and returning each day. Whenever a uniformed soldier marched past the house, Schachtner would cry out and say, "Papa." In the spring of 1945, Schachtner, then seven years old, caught sight of the horse-drawn wagons piled high with the twisted remains of the camp dead as they were hauled past his house to a mass grave just outside of town. Only in his teenage years was he able to place this nightmare vision—the white gaze of the vacant eyes, the idiot gape of the starved mouths, the graceless wave of these skeletal arms as they rose and fell with each wagon lurch—in a moral and historical context. At the age of seventeen, Schachtner left his family and Dachau, moving first to Switzerland, then to Spain, and eventually to Paraguay, only to return to Dachau ten years later. Though the demands of family life and his profession, graphic design and bookmaking, have to a large extent determined the course of his career, Schachtner also concedes that darker forces may have initially compelled him to leave and ultimately to return to Dachau. "Once Dachau is in you, you can never escape it," Schachtner says.

Several years ago, these same spirits visited Martin Zaidenstadt. They found an elderly man living in contented retirement in a comfortable two-story home on a peaceful tree-lined street with a bus stop at the end of the block. Like millions of other Holocaust survivors, Martin Zaidenstadt had emerged from the gates of a concentration camp in the first months of 1945 with little more than his life, the striped uniform on his back, and the experience gained from four years of survival in the franchised horror of the Final Solution. That summer he had returned to Poland—in a borrowed American jeep, he claims—only to discover that virtually his entire family had perished. With rumors abounding that Poles were quietly murdering returning Jews, Martin decided to make Dachau his home. He found a job, married a German woman, and brought three children into this world. Unwilling to burden his family with the horrors of his own past, he discarded his Jewish identity, befriended the locals, including former SS guards who became his drinking buddies, and regularly attended the Catholic church down the street from their home. Martin says neither his wife, nor any of his three children, two of whom are now physicians, have ever visited the barbed-wire complex on the other side of town where Martin spent the most memorable years of his life. Until recently, Martin himself rarely stepped foot into the former concentration camp. Like most Holocaust survivors, he was too busy with the everyday business of work and family to bother with the past.

On occasion, though, the past visits Martin. In the blackest hours of the night, when he and his wife lie deep in suburban sleep, the phone rings, exploding the silence with three, four, five piercing shots into the heart of Martin's domestic tranquility. He lurches from his bed, stumbling, sleep-soaked, through the darkened house to seize the phone. The past hangs on the line, either in a long silence or a deeply taken breath, or it whispers through the receiver, "We know who you are. We know where you live."

Like a mystical incantation, the words conjure up the spirit of the Jew Martin thought he had left across town behind the barbed wire of the former concentration camp. And suddenly, the survivor stands alone in the night in Germany, with his German wife in his bed, and his German children asleep in their rooms, and the German neighbors and the German police, and Martin, the Polish Jew, stands alone in Dachau clutching the phone. They know who he is, they know where he lives. But Martin will not perish like his mother and father and uncles and aunts or like the millions of other Jews of Europe. He knows how to care for himself. Martin has, as I well know, a gun in his desk. "I survived the Nazis," he tells me. "I will survive the neo-Nazis."

Other voices, the voices of the departed comrades,

have also called Martin, and undone the domestic peace he had enjoyed for nearly a half-century. They have driven him from his home, through the cobblestone streets of Dachau and east beyond where the former concentration camp stretches itself across the green fields of the Dachau moorland. Each day, like a man possessed, Martin dons his coat and cap, clutches a black nylon satchel with a banana and a roll of crackers, and sets off for the camp—walking to the bus stop at the end of his street and taking Bus 726 directly to the stop nearest the camp. It is here outside the brick extermination facility in the camp's far northeast corner that Martin Zaidenstadt finds his peace.

I first encountered Martin at the camp on a bitter January day in 1996. I had brought my father and several visitors to Dachau to tour the camp and afterward to stroll through the old town. As we entered the tree-lined area that houses Baracke X, the official designation for the extermination unit, I directed my group to the far end of the building, explaining that the compound was originally entered from the west rather than the south. Visitors, I told them, walk directly into the crematorium room rather than entering the building, as intended, through the disinfectant stalls, into the undressing and holding rooms, and finally into the gas chamber—disguised as a shower—beyond which stand the crematory ovens.

"You are right," I heard someone say, and turned to see an elderly man standing beside us. He was wearing a tweed hat with ear warmers, and a heavy coat. "My name is Martin Zaidenstadt. I come here every day for fifty years." He went on to say that he was a Holocaust survivor and that after his liberation from the camp he remained in Dachau. When I told him that I occasionally wrote about Dachau, he gave me his name, address, and phone number, and told me I should call on him the next time I was in town.

3

LUDWIKA ZAIDENSTADT IS REMARKABLY tolerant of the journalistic riffraff her husband occasionally brings home from the gas chamber. A slender woman with a kind smile and luminescent white hair that wraps her head like a halo, she offers a cup of coffee, a glass of apple juice, a light snack, knowing full well that her husband, who for so many decades devoted himself to his family and his career, has become an object of curious fascination to these foreign reporters.

Martin has invited me over this morning to discuss his campaign to break Dachau's conspiracy of silence about the gas chamber. For the last few years, Martin has verbally accosted tour guides who have promoted the "lie" that the gas chamber was never put into operation. Historians insist there is no evidence the Dachau gas chamber was ever used. Martin insists otherwise. Standing outside the gas-chamber door, he has sought to enlighten individual visitors and organized tour groups. For his efforts he has been reprimanded by Barbara Distel, the director of the memorial site and archives. "She was only three years old when I was in the camp," Martin fumes. "What does she know? I am telling the truth. I know what I am saying is true because I saw it with my own eyes. Martin always tells the truth."

His voice simmers with the fiery determination of the self-righteous.

We are seated in his "office," a converted bedroom at the back of the house, littered with the tools of his former trade—an independent finance and brokering service. A dusty manual typewriter sits on a filing cabinet beside a tattered *Aktenordner* with documents dating from the late 1970s. A plastic pen holder from the Dachau *Volksbank* sits on his pressed-wood-and-veneer desk; a faded Mercedes-Benz poster displaying a full range of passenger and service vehicles blankets the scarred wall.

"Look at this," Martin says, handing me a letter from Max Mannheimer, a prominent concentration camp survivor and chairman of the International Dachau Committee, the official organization representing thousands of Dachau survivors. I know Max Mannheimer, an elegant and kind gentleman who lives in a suburb east of Munich. The letter is dated February 3, 1995. As I peruse the letter, Martin orders me to read aloud.

"Dear Martin Zaidenstadt," I begin. "I know that you have had a difficult time, and I value you and always enjoy seeing you. Nevertheless, I must urgently request that you not interfere in the tours that are being conducted at the memorial site by the various professional guides."

"See!" Martin interrupts. "What did I tell you?" When I pause and look at him, he nods at me gravely to continue reading. "It was reported to me that you took aside the teacher from one school class and told him that the special guides from the Ministry of Culture were providing incorrect information. This is not acceptable and damages not only the reputation of the memorial site but also the memory of the dead as well as the survivors." In firm but gentle language Mannheimer asks Martin to refrain from disrupting the tours and disturbing the visitors with his stories. As I read, Martin lights an HB cigarette, all the while staring at me intently, following every word.

"You see! You see!" he fumes when I have finished, waving his cigarette in the air. "They want to silence me. I tell the truth. Martin always tells the truth. Look at all the letters I have received."

Martin points to a jumble of correspondence. There are letters without envelopes, and envelopes without letters, as well as any number of personal bills and diverse promotional brochures, the glossy detritus that washes in daily on the rising tide of German consumerism. Next to the pile is an ashtray overflowing with spent cigarettes. Martin hands me an opened envelope that contains one sheet of paper, the second page of a handwritten letter.

"What do you have there now?" he asks.

"It is only half a letter."

"Read it," he barks.

"At that instant, the horror of the Nazi regime hit me," I read the scrawled text. "Engineers had to have designed these artifices with the full knowledge of what they were to be used for. Draftsmen had to have prepared the specifications so that others would have known how to make them. Purchasing agents and fabricators had to have discussed and negotiated to make them, and they could not have been confused with any legitimate products. Skilled workers had to make them, others to pack and ship them, others to receive and store them, and ultimately men had to imbed them in the concrete from which they projected—these apparently innocent but fiendish devices intended only to lure victims into that place without resistance so that they could be slaughtered and burned. Those Germans whom I had shot, all had participated in some aspect of the Nazi atrocities and none were now 'innocent civilians' who had simply failed to object to these crimes. Remorse disappeared from my mind for my actions from that time on. Today, I proudly show the medals and decorations awarded for my service, and my conscience is as clear as yours must be. I doubt that our paths will ever cross again, but I am pleased to know that you found a way to make a living from the place where so many received only a terrible death. Good luck and sleep well. I am ever more one of your American friends."

"That's the gas, isn't it?" Martin says.

"Excuse me?"

"Smashed up and destroyed where the gas came in, from where it came in. That was right after the liberation. That's what I told you." He pauses and asks, "Where is he from?"

"Florida."

"What is his name?"

"Henry Kopnik."

"No, that isn't the one. It is another." He murmurs impatiently, handing me another letter. "If you read this you will see that what I am saying is true."

I look at the envelope.

"Where is it from?" he asks.

Cottonwood Court, North Dakota, I read. February 1995.

"I get them from Sweden. From all over the world. What does he write?"

The envelope contains a newspaper clipping from a newspaper called *The Good Life: Daily News*, Wahpeton, North Dakota. The article recounts the story of an eighteen-year-old North Dakota science student who visited Berlin, where he chipped off a piece of the Berlin Wall; Prague, where he attended the agricultural displays of "Expo 95"; and finally Dachau, where he met Martin Zaidenstadt, who made "*Schindler's List* become very real." Another envelope contains an article from the *Deggendorfer Zeitung*, a local north German newspaper, which recounted Martin Zaidenstadt's stories of gas chambers, crematoria, mass graves, mass executions, and medical experiments. "One question we kept asking ourselves was: Why does Herr Zaidenstadt continue to occupy himself with the horrors that he experienced? He answered this question without us even asking. 'Why do I do this? When I am here and I talk, I don't have as much time to think about what happened.' Nevertheless, it struck us: the more Martin Zaidenstadt spoke, the more he changed. By the end his voice was very tense. 'I want to explain the way it was!' He repeated this sentence again and again, completely lost in thought. As we left the memorial site, we realized that some things are better left unsaid. Sometimes words are simply not enough."

Martin is silent for a moment, stares into the distance, then reaches across his desk and hands me another letter. I look at it and hand it back.

"That is the letter from Max Mannheimer," I say.

"No, it isn't."

"Yes, it is."

"Just read it!" His expression darkens.

"Dear Martin Zaidenstadt, I know that you . . ."

Martin snatches the letter from my hand and gives me another one. And so it goes, an endless back-and-forth of letters and words, a hapless rummaging through the pile of correspondence on his desk. At one point, he hands me an advertisement for Commerzbank; at another, a promotional flyer for vacations in Greece. For the most part, though, I read him heartfelt letters from people he has met at the camp. Many of them include photographs of their authors standing with Martin beside the statue of the unknown survivor. Throughout, Martin sits and smokes, letting the words wash over him, occasionally insisting that I read entire letters, entire articles, a second, even a third time. It is both touching and tedious and pathetic, and as I sit there, indulging this man in the words of people whose lives he has touched in profound and moving ways, I wonder why his wife puts up with intruders like me.

After nearly two hours Martin glances at the wall clock. It is nearly eleven o'clock. He rises from his chair, informing me that it has gotten late and asking me if I can drive him to the camp. By this time of day, there will be a lot of people at the crematorium and gas chamber. He needs to be there.

On Martin's instructions, I drive through his neighborhood until we reach a four-lane artery that skirts the
old town, taking us out across the Dachau moorlands.
The first buds are appearing on the trees, creating a
gentle, verdant haze in the distant woods. Off to the left
is a single dramatic rise in the land, a bold granite abut-
ment pleated with the red-tile roofs of houses that cluster at its base and cling to the steep slopes, a village, it
would seem, from a Brueghel or a Dürer landscape.
This is the town of Dachau, whose summit is dominated
by the onion-dome tower of St. Jakob's, and the Dachau
Schloss, an eighteenth-century palace as cheerful and
ornate as a wedding cake, with a splay of windows that
glint brilliantly in the spring-morning sunlight. Looking across the moorlands toward the old town, it is easy
to understand the charm that transformed Dachau into
one of Germany's most vibrant artist colonies at the
turn of the last century. Emil Nolde learned to paint in
Dachau; Rainer Maria Rilke, whose daughter summered
here, used to pass pleasant evenings reading his verse in
the summer garden of the Dachau painter Carl Olof
Petersen.

As we pass the intersection of the Schleißheimer and
Alte Römer streets, the untethered moorlands gave way
to commercial clutter, a Peugeot dealer, a beverage dis-
tributor, a building-supply store, an erotic-massage par-
lor, a McDonald's, and, a bit farther down the road, the
site of the former concentration camp, known among
the historically sensitive as the *Gedenkstätte*, the memorial site, but generally referred to by locals simply as
the *KZ*—pronounced *kah-zet*—or *Lager*, the camp. Just

before the memorial site parking lot, Martin instructs me to keep driving. As I pass the first watchtower, the camp's twelve-foot wall obliterates the left-side view, leaving only the swath of white concrete and blue sky, two monochrome surfaces, one white, the other deep blue, with four simple strands of barbed wire rippling between them, a Mondrian view of the world.

At the second watchtower, where the wall has been breached for a service entrance, Martin instructs me to turn left. I obey, and find myself stopped before a red-and-white-striped barrier, the type that marks national borders and railroad crossings. Beyond lies the vast expanse of the former concentration camp, punctuated with groups of grim-faced visitors. I look at Martin as if to say, what next, nurturing a dim hope that he will thank me for the lift, open the door, and walk into the camp. Instead, he instructs me to press the button on the intercom and say that I am bringing Martin to the gas chamber. My hesitation to drive into the camp, where hundreds of reverent visitors tread silently across the cruel gravel expanse, is matched only by my discomfort at uttering the words Martin has commanded me to speak. I am to take this aging Polish Jew to the Dachau gas chamber. I look to Martin and try to gauge the seriousness of his intent. "Tell them you are bringing Martin to the gas chamber," he repeats. I roll down the window and do as instructed.

"Ich bringe Martin zur Gaskammer."

There is a metallic click. As the barrier rises and the car rolls across the gravel *Appellplatz*, Martin smiles. We have entered his domain.

4

"Maybe Martin Zaidenstadt isn't crazy at all. Maybe any normal person would go out of his mind living in Dachau." Thomas Soyer sips his Fanta as we watch a young mother in a miniskirt bump a baby carriage across the cobblestone street. "Maybe you have to be out of your mind to live normally in a place like this."

Soyer and I are seated in wickered comfort at one of the six curbside tables at Café Teufelhart in downtown Dachau. Cars roll by, their tires rumbling softly on the cobblestones. At a table next to us, an elderly man reads a newspaper, nursing a beer, and tending only occasionally to his cigar which smoulders in an ashtray. At another table, four girls from Australia, with nylon backpacks parked beside their chairs, express astonishment that after touring the concentration camp, they are "actually" sitting here in the middle of Dachau drinking Coca-Cola and eating ice cream. They revel in their astonishment for a few minutes before turning their attention to adventures that lie ahead—the Munich Hofbräuhaus that afternoon, the overnight train to Prague at nine forty-five. Meanwhile, Marina Teufelhart, the dervish wife of the proprietor, dashes in and out of the café, taking and delivering orders, chatting with customers, occasionally leaning out the second-floor window, through a burst of red geraniums, to call down to a customer at a streetside table. "Did you want that with or without a salad?" She is in her thirties, a woman of bulk and bosom who abandoned a career as a dentist in Berlin to follow her heart to Dachau, where she married Willy Teufelhart.

Café Teufelhart, situated in one of the oldest buildings in Dachau—"There has been a fire in the hearth since Columbus discovered your country," Marina tells me—has been home to the Teufelhart family for the last 125 years. For four generations the Teufelharts have sold baked goods to the people of Dachau, and for a brief lucrative stretch in this century supplied the Nazi concentration camp and its inmates with their daily bread.

Ten years ago, when Willy inherited the bakery, he and Marina cleared the second-floor rooms of their personal belongings, installed a kitchen and bar, and transformed it into a café. With its bare wood floors and creaky staircase, it has retained all the charm and domesticity of its years as a residence. It feels lived in. The walls are hung with paintings by contemporary Dachau artists. Near the coatrack is a pile of back issues of *Der Spiegel*, *Stern*, and *Focus*, as well as dog-eared copies of *Playboy*. Marina has something for everyone. She serves the best French onion soup and the only macrobiotic salad in town. On Friday and Saturday nights, Willy organizes poetry readings, jazz concerts, and occasionally "unplugged" rock concerts by local bands. You come to Café Teufelhart when you're hungry or thirsty, or just need some pampering from Marina, or to catch up on the local town gossip.

I come to Café Teufelhart for Thomas Soyer. For the last seven years, Soyer has covered the "Dachau beat" for the *Süddeutsche Zeitung*, one of Germany's leading daily newspapers. His articles generally appear in the newspaper's local edition, the *Dachauer Neueste*, but will be picked up by the parent paper when there is noteworthy news in Dachau—the desecration of a Jewish grave, an epithet scrawled on the camp wall, a major scandal by a local artist. In 1996, Soyer's work leaped into international headlines when he reported on a tiff between Barbara Distel, head of the concentration camp memorial site, and Roland Kramer, manager of the local McDonald's. In the spring of '96, Kramer, who ran the McDonald's in Würzburg before coming to Dachau, and claims to have introduced the first drive-thru in Germany—dubbed "McDrive"—launched an advertising campaign aimed at the "concentration camp tourist." With almost a million people visiting the former camp each year and nothing but a bratwurst stand for competition, the Dachau McDonald's, which was less than a mile from the camp, had the potential to become one of the most lucrative fast-food places on the Continent. That spring, Kramer designed a handbill and assigned one of his employees to place copies under the windshield wipers of cars in the parking lot next to the memorial site. The flyer provided a map from the parking lot to the restaurant and an accompanying text in German and somewhat stilted English:

Dear visitor,
welcome to Dachau
welcome to McDonald's

Our restaurant got 120 seats, about 40
outdoor seats and for our young guests an
Indoor-, and an Outdoor Playland.

How to find us?
Really simple. Just follow the picture!
We're happy for your visit!

Your McDonald's Restaurant Dachau

After spending three hours wandering the grounds
of the former concentration camp with their children,
after viewing the barbed wire, the watchtowers, and the
gas chamber, the visitors—so Kramer reasoned—would
welcome the opportunity to sit down in a clean, cheerful
atmosphere, rest their weary feet, and have something
warm to eat. In good weather, their children could play
on the outdoor plastic slide; in bad weather, there was a
playroom with a Ronald McDonald figure and a large
bin filled with colorful plastic balls. The promotion
campaign attracted not only the attention of the visitors
but also of Barbara Distel, who found the promotion
"tasteless" and "inappropriate." Distel sent Kramer a
letter of complaint, and a copy to Soyer, who in turn
wrote an article. "Fast-food advertising isn't always in
the best taste, at least that is the case with the Dachau
McDonald's owner," Soyer wrote in a strongly worded

article that chronicled Kramer's sins and Distel's distress. Within a day the story was screaming from headlines across Germany, and causing concern at corporate headquarters outside Chicago. Overnight, Kramer became the best-known McDonald's manager in all Europe. With news of the scandal reverberating in corporate headquarters, McDonald's went into damage-control mode. In a meeting with Ignatz Bubis, head of the German Jewish Community, the CEO of McDonald's Germany offered a formal apology, agreed to make a financial contribution to a local organization associated with the memorial site, and promised not to post any advertisements within five hundred meters of the former concentration camp. When I asked one Dachauer how they had come up with the five-hundred-meter no-advertising zone around the former concentration camp, he shrugged his shoulders. "I guess Bubis was having a five-hundred-meter day."

On this particular afternoon, Tom Soyer has new adventures to report. He has just returned from Israel, where he accompanied Kurt Piller, Dachau's new thirty-eight-year-old mayor, on a controversial visit. In a stormy town meeting at which Piller announced his plans to visit the Jewish state, Gertrud Schmidt-Podolsky, a blond political firebrand, rose to her feet and declared that he had no right to represent the town of Dachau in Israel, that without approval by the Town Council he had to go as an ordinary citizen, and at his own expense. Thea Zimmer, another Council member, stood up and declared, "Ich habe noch ein bißchen Stolz, deutsch zu sein"—"I still have a bit of pride being German." In

Israel, Piller engaged in exactly the sort of penance that many townspeople had feared. In Jerusalem he stood grimly before the Wailing Wall, shared tears with Holocaust survivors at Yad Vashem, and drove to the outskirts of Jerusalem, where he committed his town to creating the "Dachau Woods" by symbolically planting one of what he promised would be thousands of trees to follow.

As Soyer recounts his journey with Piller through Israel, Marina Teufelhart first takes our order, then after it has been served, returns repeatedly to urge Soyer to eat his meal before it gets cold. She wants to know if there is anything wrong with it. Does it need to be reheated? Would he prefer something else? When it begins to drizzle, she leans out the upstairs window and encourages us to bring our lunch inside. But it is a warm spring afternoon, and the light rain feels good on our cheeks. Soyer's narrative is repeatedly interrupted by passersby who stop to greet him, or Teufelhart regulars who exchange news about the latest political intrigue in town. After seven years on the Dachau beat, Soyer knows just about everyone and everything in Dachau. Though he adamantly insists on his status as a journalist rather than a historian, he has probed through his work into the darkest and most painful corners of Dachau's past. I am therefore surprised that he has never heard of Martin Zaidenstadt. He is surprised as well. He picks at his salad before looking me in the eye and asking, "Are you sure he is for real?"

Soyer is a lean man of thirty with sharp, probing eyes, close-cut dark hair, and a silver stud in his left ear. Having spent time in Dachau unraveling the machinations of small-town politics, he has become cautious of just about everything. I assure Soyer that Martin is very much for real. I have been visiting him on and off for the last few years, and it does not matter when I go to the former concentration camp, be it in the early morning when the camp first opens or late in the day, Martin is always there, in the blazing heat of summer, on the bitterest days of January, bundled in a wool coat and scarf with his hat pulled low over his ears, a black nylon satchel with a banana and crackers slung over his shoulder, like a lone sentinel, inclined slightly forward propped on his cane, in front of the crematorium. When his legs give out, he sits on a nearby bench. He is always there. "Thomas," I say, "I don't think you fake something like that."

"I didn't say he was faking it," Soyer replies. "I asked you if you are sure he is for real." Soyer then tells me the story of a certain Gloria. Several years ago, a group of Germans visited Auschwitz with Aktion Sühnezeichen— Action Repentance—a religious group that organizes pilgrimages to former concentration and death camps for guilt-ridden Germans. Among their number was a pregnant woman who was known as an *Auschwitz Kind,* one of the thousands of children liberated from Auschwitz after the war. Many children had been tattooed, on their arms when there was enough meat on their bones, on their thighs when not. Through these tattooed numbers, relief agencies after the war were able to trace the origins of these orphans and to provide them, later in life, with brief sketches of their past. Many children, however, emerged from the death camps without markings or memories. Their pasts remained black holes. Gloria was one such *Auschwitz Kind.* Now, as a grown woman who was about to give birth to a child of her own, she had returned to this place of horror to try to piece together fragments of childhood memory. She recalled in great detail images of the Warsaw Ghetto, the fact that she lived on the "Aryan side" outside the Ghetto and that she used to smuggle food and other things to the beleaguered Jewish community behind the walls. She could not recall the circumstances under which she had come to Auschwitz, nor whether she had been transported with friends or acquaintances. But she did recall that she had been brought to Birkenau, officially known as Auschwitz II, the vast extermination facility two kilometers east of the original concentration camp, Auschwitz I.

The group of German penitents who arrived in Auschwitz was met by Tadeusz Szymanski, a member of the Auschwitz memorial site staff who had devoted his career to interviewing and working with the surviving children of Auschwitz. Knowing that Gloria was pregnant, and that the encounter with the site of her childhood horror could be traumatic, Szymanski advised Gloria not to go on the tour. She insisted, nevertheless, on seeing both Auschwitz I and Birkenau. During the tour of Auschwitz I, a former Polish military caserne consisting of sixty or so brick barracks, Gloria seemed fine, asking Szymanski many questions about the facility. Yet during the subsequent tour of Birkenau, with its railway tracks and infamous "ramp," where children were separated from fathers and mothers, with the shattered ruins of its concrete gas chambers—dynamited just days before liberation—with its desolate vistas of crumbling brick chimneys where the wooden barracks once stood, Gloria spoke not a word. She walked through the camp focusing intensely on every word Szymanski said, as if seeking some detail that would unlock the memories of her time spent here. Afterward, Gloria recounted her story for the camp archive. On the tape recording, she speaks compellingly and without hesitation, only occasionally pausing to find the right word. Several months after the visit, however, Szymanski received a letter from Gloria begging for forgiveness. Everything she said about herself during the visit to Auschwitz had been fabricated. Not only had she never been in Birkenau, Soyer tells me, it turned out that she had not even been born until after the war. "There are some people who have read and seen so much about the Holocaust that they begin to confuse themselves with the victims," Soyer observes. "It wouldn't surprise me if your friend Martin were one of these people." He falls silent and stares at me to see how the idea registers.

Suddenly a voice calls from above. Marina Teufelhart is leaning out the second-floor window. "Cappuccino or espresso?" She stands there for an instant, smiling brilliantly, her full bosom pouring out over the box of bright red geraniums.

5

"My name is Martin Zaidenstadt. I survived the camp. I come here every day for fifty-three years." Martin holds up a block of business cards wrapped with a rubber band. The cards have his name, address, and phone number. He turns the block around to display a plastic card of the 42nd Division of the United States Army, the unit that liberated the Dachau Concentration Camp on April 29, 1945. Along the bottom of the card are the words *Freedom Freiheit Liberté*. Three arched bars of yellow, red, and green grace the top. "Rainbow Division. See? They liberate me from camp. I come here every day for last fifty-three years."

Four Americans, two sisters from Texas, each with a boyfriend, one with a baseball cap and a video camera slung around his neck, the other a tall man with a Jamaican accent who currently resides in Colorado, all of them Baha'i on a missionary tour of Europe, gape at Martin.

"You were in here?" the Jamaican asks.

"Three and a half years I live here," Martin says solemnly, holding out his card like a credential. There follows a moment of uncomfortable silence. The Americans stare at Martin, then exchange bewildered glances. This is not the sort of encounter you have in Port

Arthur, Texas, or Golden, Colorado. This is not even the sort of European experience that *Let's Go* or *The Rough Guide* or even *Michelin* prepares you for. Advice on when to drink bottled water, how to use a Turkish toilet, or how much to tip a German waiter, yes, but what to say when you find yourself standing before a four-cylinder vented crematory oven, face-to-face with a man whom Adolf Hitler had meant to gas, incinerate, and send up the brick chimney in a cloud of blue smoke? The Europeans, who have so finely honed the etiquette of arrival, a *Handkuss* with a click of the heels in Austria, a *busse* on each cheek in France, three real kisses to the cheek—left, right, left—in the Netherlands, and nothing more than a brisk handshake—as chilly as a London fog—across the Channel in England, have yet to develop a protocol for greeting Holocaust survivors in front of a former extermination facility.

The four Americans stare at Martin, then glance at one another, shifting uncomfortably from one foot to the other, searching their hearts and minds for the "right thing" to say. As the collective discomfort deepens, the Jamaican's face suddenly brightens. Looking Martin straight in the eye, he smiles, swings his arm in a wide arc, like a politician winding up for the shake, and locks hands with Martin.

"Well," he sputters, placing his trust in purity of heart, "congratulations, sir." There follows an instant of hesitation as he awaits Martin's reaction, and then a look of exuberance as Martin returns the smile. So this is how it is done. The other three join in, each in turn, taking Martin's hand, shaking it vigorously, and offering heartfelt congratulations on his having survived the gas chamber and crematory ovens of Dachau. For the four American tourists, it is the encounter of a lifetime. For Martin it is just another day on the safe side of the gas chamber door.

It is Sunday morning in Dachau. For the last two decades, nearly a million visitors a year have traveled to this place of horror. They tour the permanent photo exhibition located in the former SS administration building, they walk through reconstructed barracks, and swing the wrought-iron gate with the inscription ARBEIT MACHT FREI—Work Liberates—on its sturdy hinges until it clanks shut. They then walk the quarter-mile promenade, the seemingly endless rows of vacant barrack foundations on their right and left, the running walls of concrete, barbed wire, and watchtowers. The gravel crunches underfoot. It is like walking on crushed brittle bones.

In the camp's northwest corner, a wooden bridge crosses a modest stream and leads one into an open area encircled by trees and occupied by two one-story red-brick buildings with black peaked roofs. Except for the oversize square brick chimneys, the two buildings could pass for gingerbread houses from a children's fairytale book. The smaller building houses two crematory ovens. Both contain residual ash, which, in humid weather, fills the dank space. You feel compelled to take short, shallow breaths. Or not to breathe at all. The larger building is home to Europe's first comprehensive extermination facility—a set of delousing chambers followed by two windowless rooms that lead to a green steel door, with rills for holding rubber seals. Behind the door, with still swings easily on its hinges, is a dark, tight space marked BRAUSEBAD—Shower—with a dozen shower funnels bored into the ceiling. A sign in five languages indicates that the gas chamber was never put into operation. A second metal door, also with rills for rubber seals, leads into a hall whose peaked ceilings and large crossbeams give it the feeling of a ski chalet, and enough space to generously accommodate the four massive brick crematory ovens, each one nearly ten feet in height. An adjacent room was used as a holding room for unburned corpses.

It is just outside this building that Martin Zaidenstadt holds his daily vigil as he has done, so he claims, for a half-century, but which, by my count, has been for the past five years. Like the disclaimer in the gas chamber, the facts of the case don't really seem to matter; the very presence of the gas chamber and Martin are a testament unto themselves.

Martin has arrived at nine o'clock sharp this particular Sunday, and except for a brief lunch—a banana, some crackers—he has been greeting people who enter the open area between the two crematoria buildings. Depending on his mood, and the appearance of his audience, he speaks English, German, Polish, Spanish, Italian, Yiddish, or Hebrew. The routine is always the same: his name, his status as a survivor, his liberation by the Rainbow Division, his half-century vigil in front of the camp, and a brief tour either of the gas chamber or the crematory ovens, though usually not both. Occasionally, Martin opens his wallet and unfolds a tattered article about him that appeared two years ago in the *New York Times*. Generally, the encounters conclude with a photo-op beside the statue of the unknown survivor.

Martin likes the group of four Americans and takes them first to the gas chamber, where he explains that he saw with his own eyes hundreds of human beings led to the gas chamber, that he knew the attendants who slammed and locked the doors, that he heard the screams. He shows them the shafts for venting the gas chamber, and the observation ports through which the SS could observe the effects of the poison gas.

In the crematorium area, Martin, to the astonishment of his charges as well as the thirty or so visitors on a guided tour, steps over the rope barrier and walks to one of the crematory ovens. He begins to explain the venting and firing chambers, then grabs the sliding tray on which the bodies were placed, rams it into the oven, pulls it out, and demonstrates how it can be tipped to dump the remaining ash and bones. As Martin works the oven with erratic angular gestures, like a man possessed, the others look on with a mixture of horror and astonishment. Three times, the Texan brings the video camera to his face to film, then lowers it.

"Can I take your picture?" he asks when Martin has finished.

"No, not here," Martin says. "Come, I show you where. I no charge for pictures. Pictures free."

He leads them outside the building to a life-size casting in patinaed bronze that depicts an emaciated inmate, his arms hanging limply at his sides. Martin poses with the two girls while the two men take photographs.

"You send me copy?" Martin says afterward.

"Of course," one of the women replies. "What is your address?"

Martin pulls out his block of cards and hands her one. When she thanks him, he hesitates and murmurs, "Cards are expensive in Germany." As she puts the card in her purse, Martin adds, "I charge no money for photographs, but I must pay for my own cards. One hundred fifty marks for six hundred. Very expensive."

"Of course." Smiling at him with genuine sympathy, the woman reaches into her purse, removes a dollar, and presses it into his hand. Martin takes the dollar, flattens it with his fingers, studies it closely, then says to her, "This is little." An uncomfortable silence ensues. The woman looks at the Jamaican, who nods. She reaches into her wallet again and hands Martin a five-dollar bill. When Martin tries to return the single, she gently presses it back into his hand, and whispers, "Keep it."

6

LOST IN A MEMORY that consumes her attention like a deep-night dream, Else Hirschberger stares at the photo album, her eyes moist with tears. For the past forty-five minutes we have sat on the sofa paging through an album pasted with photographs, birth announcements, death notices, and an occasional yellowed newspaper clipping from the 1920s and '30s. Else is a frail woman with snowy white hair who has spent virtually every day of her life in this village. She was born at home before this century began, learned to read and write in the village schoolhouse, was married at a young age in the village church, and will eventually be buried in the village cemetery. As her daughter leafs through the family photo album, pausing to explain the fates of particular relatives, Else listens intently, glancing from the photos to her daughter's face. It is clear that she has heard these stories a hundred times before, that they are the same stories she has handed down to her daughter, who is now entrusted with transporting the family history into the future.

After lingering for an especially long time over a series of baptism photographs of a cousin now married with her own children and living in Graz or Vienna or somewhere far away, the daughter turns a page and

I find myself staring at "Uncle Walther" at war. In a crisp German uniform, with a smile on his face, and a machine gun poised jauntily at his side—like some aristocrat at the conclusion of a successful day's hunt—he stands in the snow before a pile of heaped corpses. Beneath the photograph in a clear, proud hand is the inscription: *Fünfundzwanzig erledigt*. Twenty-five finished off. There follows a series of similar photographs, piles of snow-covered corpses and inscriptions registering the number of dead, with always Uncle Walther and a few comrades posed with their weapons. From the looks on their faces, it is clear they were having the time of their life.

This is not Dachau. This is Förolach, a mountain village in southern Austria, with all the accompanying pastoral trappings, a verdant valley with wooded slopes rising to snowcapped mountains, and church spires cutting cozy profiles up and down the length of the valley. Twice each day, a modest train with six wooden carriages bumping behind rattles up to Hermagor at the head of the valley, then turns around and rattles back down. This is the Gail Valley, birthplace of my grandfather, namesake of my mother, and home to my ancestors since the time when Gregor Vladimir Wernitznig was awarded a plot of land for "great bravery, courage, and clever tactics"—so the ancient document reads—while fighting some war for some Habsburg emperor somewhere in the Balkans at some point in the late seventeenth century. It must have been a modest act of heroism, for the family did not receive a title, or a coat of arms, or even a piece of land that could sustain anything more noble than a two-story stone farmhouse, called "Schuli," on a rather steep mountainside in what was then a rather obscure corner of the empire.

When my grandfather was two years old, his father was kicked in the head by a horse and died. A few years later, his older brother Vincent fell from a galloping steed, caught his foot in the stirrup, and was dragged to death. Not long after that, his mother tumbled down the back steps of the old farmhouse and broke her neck. By the age of sixteen my grandfather was an orphan and heir to this rather treacherous piece of real estate. In the spring of 1909, Uncle Tony, a distant relative who owned a bar and bowling alley in Wisconsin, visited Förolach. "Go to America, Michael," he told my grandfather. Placing the farm in the stewardship of his uncle Johann, my grandfather packed his bags and, with a cousin also named Johann, set off for America.

Now, sixty-seven years later, his grandson has returned to the family roots. My visit is celebrated like the return of a long-lost son. I am paraded through the village, wander the ruins of "Schuli," the stone farmhouse where my great-grandmother met her tragic end, and visit the few aging residents who still have flickering recollections of my grandfather. Invariably, they sit me down in an overheated kitchen, pour me a glass of homemade schnapps, and declare me to be the spitting image of young Michael Wernitznig. The ancient eyes brighten as they recall a fun-loving, spirited young man too energetic, too ambitious for this quiet mountain village, who set out for America before the First World War to find his fortune. One elderly woman tells me the

story of how one fine summer day my grandfather
mounted a bicycle, and rode straight across a farmer's
field, laughing and singing; I hear this story so many
times that I am left to wonder whether this was my
grandfather's most notable achievement in Förolach, or
whether nothing else of consequence has happened in
the intervening seventy years. With memories of my
grandfather lingering pleasantly in the air, we raise a
glass of schnapps to his memory, then pour another and
drink again to his memory. By midday I am staggering.

Now we are seated in the cozy warmth of the house
with its overstuffed chairs, antique tables, portraits on
the walls, the very heart of idyllic comfort, trying to
connect me to my roots. As we linger briefly on the
pages chronicling Uncle Walther's wartime adventures,
I ask polite questions about when and where, and am
told that it was in Norway in the winter of 1940, and am
also shown a photograph on the wall, a handsome
somber man in his dark uniform with a swastika on his
cap. I am informed that he had died five years earlier of a
heart attack. We pause for a moment. The photographs
barely seem to register with Else.

When my great-aunt turns the page, I find myself
staring at a full-page black-and-white glossy portrait
of Adolf Hitler. It is one of those congenial portraits
intended to evoke the paternal side of the Führer, a portrait of him in a suit with his hair carefully combed and
parted to the side, his distinctive mustache perfectly
trimmed, his eyes with a particularly warm intensity. It
was the kind of picture that many Germans and Aus-
trians framed and hung on living room walls, or, if

changing times demanded, removed and burned in the fireplace or relegated to the trash bin. Some families, like mine for example, chose to keep it and placed it in the family photo album for safekeeping. I could immediately sense my aunt's discomfort and, playing the good guest, I smiled at her and asked, "Ist er auch verwandt?" Is he also a relative?

At the time my reaction was as glib as my question. A passing moment in a weekend filled with memories and familial chatter. I spent the balance of the visit attending a festival, meeting neighbors and more distant cousins, and then took my leave. They escorted me onto the train and waved me off, not unlike the day when my grandfather departed two generations earlier.

But a decade and a half later, wandering the streets of Dachau, trying to ascertain and judge the relationship of the guilt of the people of Dachau to the crimes of the Holocaust, and wondering how they could live with themselves and with their memories, the image of my great-aunt and my mother's cousin and Uncle Walther with his piles of bodies and Adolf Hitler came to me. I recalled that family photo album sitting on a bookshelf in Förolach and wondered what connection, if any, it had to me. If I could not be held accountable for the actions or political beliefs of my relatives, what, I wondered, was in fact my personal moral connection to the bloody crimes of these blood relatives? Of course, I knew, children inherit the sins of their parents, but how far did this genealogy of guilt extend, to aunts and uncles and cousins, two, three, or four times removed, and a half a world away?

7

Clutch the fish-shaped brass handle to St. Jakob's, pull open the heavy-seated door, and enter the cool, bright space of Dachau's Renaissance church. Dip your hand into the cool chill of holy water and moisten your forehead, sternum, and chest in the sign of the cross as you pay homage to the Father, Son, and Holy Ghost. Inhale the incense, bow to the two skeletons of Dachau's eighteenth-century bishops lying in state behind glass cases on either side of the altar, and kneel, at the rear of the church, before the gleaming white and blue enameled statue of the Virgin Mary with seven gold swords plunged violently into her bleeding heart. The Mother of Seven Sorrows.

This is where pious Dachauers come to attend mass, receive communion, and seek absolution for their sins. Every week, from his confessional at St. Jakob's, a dark wooden box in the glorious white splendor of St. Jakob's, Father Kanzler dispenses salvation in small and large doses. A handful of Hail Marys and Our Fathers for using God's name in vain; an hour of prayer and meditation for wishing illness upon one's teacher; five rosaries every night for a month for coveting another's job or spouse or model-year BMW. But Father Kanzler knows of no prayer, no baptism that can cleanse the "original sin" of having been born in Dachau, except, of course, to have your child delivered in a Munich hospital.

"How many cases like this?" Father Kanzler muses early one afternoon in his chancery office as he leans back in his chair. "I cannot tell you exactly how many, but certainly there is a surprisingly large number. It is not uncommon that I am asked to baptize a child and when I look at the birth certificate see that it was born in Munich. The parents are from Dachau, have lived their entire lives in Dachau, but they take the child to Munich so that it will not have 'Dachau' on its birth certificate." Father Kanzler pauses for a moment, then adds, "It is like the mark of Cain." Father Kanzler is a pleasant-looking man in his early fifties who has the stoutness of a friar with a ring of curly gray locks and a broad, kind smile. Having joined the priesthood at age twenty, Kanzler studied theology in Munich, then tended to a number of parishes in and around Munich. He loved his work, providing moral guidance for the young, receiving the sincere penance that came with the introspection of old age. In 1992 the bishop of Munich approached Kanzler with the idea of transferring from his parish in Oberhaching to Dachau. Although Kanzler had not listed Dachau as one of the parishes to which he had wished to be transferred, it seems that no one else had either. With Father Hausl, St. Jakob's priest for ten years, about to assume responsibilities in a different parish, Kanzler agreed to take the job.

When I ask Kanzler if his pastoral duties in Dachau differ at all from those in other communities, he insists that they do not. Like other towns in Bavaria, he tells me, Dachau is predominantly Roman Catholic, with a loyal group of parishioners who regularly attend Sunday mass and participate in church-related activities. There is a "women's circle" that meets once each week, a Bible discussion every Thursday, and an extremely active youth club. Last year they organized a fund-raising disco at the August Volksfest. This past spring, twenty young Dachauers took a trip to Rome, where they had an audience with the Pope. His parish, Kanzler insists, is a parish like any other parish, and bears no more guilt for the Nazi crimes than any other place in Germany.

It is hard for me to believe that a man who has devoted his life to the spirit has not been visited by the tens of thousands of spirits that haunt every corner of this town. I tell Kanzler that I do not believe that Dachau is like other towns. What other town has a gas chamber and a crematorium and a mass grave for the unidentified remains of thirty thousand tangled corpses? Dachau may seem like a town like any other town to the people who live here, but to the rest of the world it is a place of atrocity and horror. When I finish, he concedes that from the outside Dachau is perceived differently, noting that when he attends gatherings of religious leaders and says that he is the parish priest in Dachau, his colleagues of the cloth take note. They listen more closely to his words. "Does this heightened visibility," I ask, "bring with it a greater responsibility?"

"The burden is greater but the guilt is not greater," he replies.

"And what about the responsibility?"

For the first time in our conversation he pauses to reflect. After a moment he says, "That is a difficult question," then falls silent. I watch this man of God struggling for the first time, it would seem, with the meaning of this place called Dachau. He looks at me, shakes his head, and says, "Ich weiß nicht." He doesn't know. I press him, asking if God possibly had something special in mind when he chose Dachau. I expect him to respond that it was Himmler, not God, who made that decision. Instead he says, "Why me? Why does it have to be me? That was Job's question. That is the age-old question. Could the Dachauers have prevented the concentration camp? Could the Germans have prevented Hitler or the Nazi atrocities, or the whole Nazi movement for that matter? We can ask ourselves these questions for eternity. A person does not live with 'what if.' A person lives with his or her own reality and comes to terms with that." He speaks of the *Kainsmal*—the mark of Cain—and the *Erbsünde*—the original sin—and finally concedes there is in fact no divine act that can cleanse Dachau's soul of this blackest of sins. Only the "baptism" of human forgiveness can grant the people of Dachau absolution, he says. He pauses, looks to see if he has satisfied me, and seems somehow more satisfied with himself. Then he adds quietly, "Vergeben heißt aber nicht vergessen." Forgiveness, however, does not mean forgetting.

8

IT ISN'T ALWAYS EASY to explain how one can live in a place like Dachau, and it often helps to have an alibi. Franz Eder, whose mother hid a Jewish girl in her house, and fed and clothed her for three years, uses the *Juden-Alibi*, as does clothing-store owner Tobias Seefried, whose father continued to buy from Jewish wholesalers, despite harassment by town Nazis, until the last of his Munich business associates was packed into a boxcar and shipped to Auschwitz. Astrid Hauser soothes her conscience with the *Kartoffel-Alibi*—as a young girl, she was sent into the street to surreptitiously leave potatoes on the edge of the sidewalk for the *Häftlinge* to drop in their pockets as they were marched through the streets. I have heard a dozen or so *Dachauer* invoke the *Sympathie-Alibi*—it was emotionally devastating to see these gaunt figures and know there was not a single thing on this God-given earth you could do to help them.

Lorenz Reitmeier, the mayor of Dachau for nearly thirty postwar years, offers the *Opfer-Alibi*—the victim alibi—which holds that Dachau residents today, like the Jews of the Nazi era, know what it is like to be despised and shunned by the world. The *Dachauer*, like the *Juden*, Reitmeier once claimed, are victims of spite and blind prejudice. The town is awash in stories of victimization—tires slashed in Switzerland, a side mirror snapped off in Croatia, a swastika scratched into the hood in Poland simply because the car license bears the telltale letters DAH. At soccer matches, kids from neighboring towns deride the Dachau teammates as "*KZler*"— pronounced *kah-zet-ler*—a derogatory acronym for a concentration camp inmate. Most of these alibis are exchanged quietly, behind closed doors, often attributed to second and third sources.

In Dachau, the local alibis are as varied as the suspicions of guilt they are intended to expunge. Some gasp for credibility; others sit as solid as a Dachau cobblestone. Take, for example, Sabine Goetz's *Brot-Alibi*. Sabine, a stately woman in her early seventies, with limpid blue eyes that still sparkle with the aquamarine light of her past beauty, is the daughter of Michael Hoflehner, whose name is preserved on a large family burial plot in the town cemetery, as well as on a main-street establishment, Bäckerei Hoflehner, across the street from Café Teufelhart. Like the Teufelharts, the Hoflehners put their ovens to work for the concentration camp, helping to keep the inmates and their keepers supplied with bread. Michael Hoflehner, a gregarious and hardworking man, not only met his contractual obligations with the SS—eight hundred loaves per day—but also risked his livelihood by delivering additional bread directly into the hands of the camp inmates. And there is evidence to prove it: letters from camp survivors expressing their gratitude for not only the physi-

cal but also the moral sustenance the Hoflehners provided. "I don't understand why you risked your life for
ours but I want you to know it is something I will never
forget," a survivor from Poland wrote in 1972. "You
allowed me to keep my faith in humanity in the worst
years of my life."

Late one morning, I call on Sabine Goetz and her
husband, Herman. They live in a handsome two-story
house with a beautifully maintained garden where late
spring flowers blaze among the bushes. An inflatable
wading pool is already set up in the garden in anticipa-
tion of the summer and their grandchildren. Sabine
loves her life in Dachau. She always has and says, with
the clear conscience of the innocent, that the years of
the Nazi occupation were among the best she can
remember.

"I was a teenager," recalls Sabine, "and every Friday
night I would put on my nicest dancing dress and go to a
movie at the Kino Universal. We'd watch a romantic
love story, and afterward we'd all go to the Café Bestler."
An impish smile crosses Sabine's face, as it invariably
does among elderly Dachau women at the mention of
Café Bestler. Café Bestler. The eyes brighten, a glow
returns to the cheeks. Café Bestler, with its rough
wooden floors, its high, gay spirits, the smoke and
drink, and, of course, the music. A three-piece band—
bass, drums, and accordion—played fast waltzes, two-
steps, and an occasional American fox trot. "In einer
kleinen Konditorei" brought everyone tumbling to the
dance floor to tango. I once turned a table of six dour

Dachau women absolutely giddy at the mere mention of Café Bestler. This is where many of today's seventy-somethings in Dachau first discovered love.

Andrea Ritter, whose father's dry-goods store—the ground floor of the family's home—stood across the street from Café Bestler, used to lie in bed as a thirteen-year-old and listen to the late-night excitement. Andrea and her three sisters, whose mother had passed away, were raised as "good Catholic girls." Though she could hear the music, the clink of glasses, and, afterward, the rap of heels and fading laughter down the empty late-night streets, she knew Café Bestler would never be a place for her. "It was not a place where nice girls went," observes Ritter, who still tends her father's shop.

When Herr Bestler—no one in Dachau can remember his first name—first set up his café and hired a local dark-haired beauty to help him tend it, the café indeed had a reputation as a rough place, where local boys scuffled with SS men for the affections of Dachau girls. But the mood mellowed with the coming of war. "All our boys were sent to the front, to Russia," Sabine Goetz recalls. "Our town was filled with nothing but tall, handsome SS men in those crisp uniforms with their shiny buttons." These were indeed not the sons of the Rastlers and the Teufelharts and the Zauners, the offspring of local farmers and shopkeepers. These were the purest of the Aryan race, hand-picked from across the Reich, from thrilling places like Berlin, Hamburg, and Cologne. And it was in Café Bestler that the Dachau girls would lose their hearts. Bestler was the place to come on a Friday night to show off a stylish dress, have a glass of wine, dance to live music, and take your pick of the finest stock of men in all Germany. "We were the luckiest girls in the Third Reich," one elderly woman told me, her eyes sparkling with the memory.

Dachau teenagers, who were too young for Café Bestler but old enough to wander the late-night streets, used to gather at the Dachau Schloss to watch Munich ablaze like a bonfire following American bombing raids, or creep stealthily along the banks of the Amper to witness the culmination of courtships begun in the rollicking confines of Café Bestler. Beside the rustling waters of the Amper, there were giggles, sighs, and promises as pure as Aryan blood. Uniform buttons glinted in the moonlight, and skirts were hoisted, exposing the white-flanked thighs to the passions of a summer night. "After the war, there were a lot of girls in Dachau with children but no husbands," Sabine told me. "We called them SS widows."

In the summer of 1942, Sabine met Herman Goetz, a handsome engineer from the Nazi construction unit known as "Organization Todt." After a "proper courtship" of six months, they were married in St. Jakob's church in Dachau. Her husband spent much of the war in France, helping strengthen the coastal defenses, and later was dispatched to Turkey. In 1940 or '41, Sabine cannot remember exactly when, her father was contracted by the SS to supply bread for the concentration camp's sick ward. Since her older brother was at war, Sabine and her younger sister delivered the bread to the camp in a small motorized cart. Eventually, as the volume of the deliveries increased, the camp began dispatching a vehicle with an SS driver, two SS guards, and three or four *Häftlinge* to pick up the bread at the bakery itself. As the war progressed and fuel became precious, they resorted to manpower: a hand-drawn sled in the winter months, a wagon when the snow cleared. Every morning around eight o'clock, the four *Häftlinge* walked up the Augsburger Strasse, two SS guards following closely behind. Generally, one guard stood watch outside while another accompanied the *Häftlinge* into the bakery. It was at this time that Sabine's father began to slip bread to the inmates, individual rolls at first, and then entire bags, which the *Häftlinge* would divide among themselves. Hoflehner was touched by the plight of the inmates with their shaved heads and striped uniforms who stomped into his shop every morning in their wooden clogs. "My father was a deeply religious man," Sabine recalls. "He always said, 'When I give someone a piece of bread, then maybe someone will do the same for my son when he is in trouble.'"

It was generally the same *Häftlinge* every day, and Sabine became fond of seeing them. She recalls one Polish inmate who always gave her a large, kind smile; another always had the latest news about developments in the war. "I don't know how he was able to get this information," she says, "but I always waited for him to arrive, to ask him about the war." According to Herman Goetz, who used to work in the bakery when he was home from the front, the SS guards generally turned a deaf ear to these exchanges, and even looked away when Hoflehner slipped the inmates the additional bread. On one occasion, during an air-raid alert, the SS guards permitted the *Häftlinge* to join them in an air-raid shelter, in violation of regulations. Huddled in a cramped subterranean space, where the Hörhammer Department Store now stands, the SS guards, their concentration camp charges, Herr Hoflehner, and his two daughters shared a freshly baked plum cake while they waited for the all-clear alarm. "I don't mean to say that they were not cruel people," says Goetz, "but for the most part the SS men in town behaved themselves. They were not all as evil as people make them out to be."

In the days immediately following the liberation of the camp, *Häftlinge* roamed the old town, plundering shops and murdering SS collaborators. In order to protect the Hoflehners out of gratitude for their support, a group of former inmates formed a cordon around the bakery and kept watch over the building. Since then, many of them have kept in regular contact with the family, sending Christmas cards, paying an occasional visit with their families. "What we did may have been dangerous, but I don't think it was especially courageous," says Goetz. "We helped those in need in the best way we could. I think any good Christian would have done the same thing." While Goetz does not wish to make too much out of his father-in-law's noble deeds, he insists that these actions have earned his family the right to live in Dachau in peace. "We love this town, and no one is going to make us feel guilty for living here," he says. "We have raised our children to be proud of Dachau, and they are doing the same with their children."

For the last hour and a half we have been sitting in the breakfast nook off the Goetzes' living room. It is a cozy space with padded wood benches and walls hung with family photographs—of birthdays and communions and vacations on Mediterranean beaches. During the course of our conversation, we are joined for a short while by one of their sons-in-law, formerly of Munich and now a proud resident of Dachau. The atmosphere is warm and inviting. When Sabine recounts her nights at Café Bestler, her voice is gay and light; it modulates to sincere compassion when she recalls the faces of the concentration camp inmates. Goetz's voice is matter-of-fact, without a trace of self-aggrandizement, when he discusses the past. But passions rise when the topic of contemporary Dachau comes up.

Goetz insists that living in Dachau is like living in any other town. He raised his children in this belief, never mentioning the existence of the concentration camp, or the role of the family bakery. Only when his children returned from school with stories of the horrors committed in their town did he and his wife recount their own family's role in this grim history. He would like to spare his grandchildren these "history lessons" altogether. "It only harms this younger generation, who had nothing to do with what happened here," Goetz says of the attempt to "burden" the younger generation with the horrors of the past. "The older generation—fine, we experienced it, we lived through it. But you should not condemn the younger generation for what we did." He pauses to stifle a rising anger, thinks better of it, then gives himself over to the moment. "At some point you have to put an end to this campaign, be it from the Jews in Israel or anywhere else. If they start with all this again and again and again . . ." His rising voice fills the room with his rage, then he cuts himself short; and though the heat of his rage quickly dissipates, his threatening words linger in the air, sinister and unsettling. I thank them for their time and literally flee the house, escaping into the crisp, clear spring air of Dachau.

9

To MY MIND, the dead of Dachau are often easier to understand than the living—especially those who died before the mid-century evils visited this picturesque village, complicating forever the notion of dying in Dachau. Back then it was easier to celebrate the living and properly mourn the dead. In the simpler one-town, one-career lives of the nineteenth century, when you grew up, worked, and died pretty much in the same place you were born, a gravestone could tell you just about everything you needed to know about someone's life.

Herr Kaspar Krebs
Tinsmith and Former Mayor
1847–1906

or

Frau Rosi Schlicht
Widow of a Schoolteacher
Served for 49 Years as Governess for the Family Schwarz
1849–1933

Herr Michael Kuffner
Local Undertaker
1859–1903

or

Frau Anna Ziegler
Born Göttler
Wife of a Local House Owner
1885–1930

I especially like the gravestones of the *Altdachauer* families, those massive tombs of stone engraved with names—Rauffer, Zauner, Hörhammer, Teufelhart, Glück, Hoflehner, Wittmann—that still lay claim to a dozen or so shops clustered around the church and the old town square. You baked your bread or sold your wares until you died, were mourned, and blessed in St. Jakob's, and then buried in the *Altfriedhof*, all within a few cobbled blocks. In Dachau you know exactly where you came from and where you were going.

Whenever I am in town, I invariably spend an hour or so wandering the *Altfriedhof* located in the Gottesacker Strasse, a three-minute walk from the Café Teufelhart. The Dachau cemetery is a tranquil, protected place surrounded by a six-foot stone wall and shaded by large oak trees whose spreading limbs provide a vaulting ceiling of green. When you enter this space, the sounds of the surrounding town seem to vanish.

I pay homage at the grave of Hermann Stockman, one of the last Dachau artists of the "golden age," whose pastoral landscapes grace the walls of the Dachau Gemäldegalerie. Though he died in 1962, his head-stone suggests the grandeur of a bygone era: "Hermann Stockmann. Royal Painter. Honorary Citizen of Dachau." His remains lie buried together with those of his wife, Lina, who died in 1957, and his daughter, Emilie, who passed away in 1986. I chuckle at the grave of Herr Martin Weinsteiger, whose gravestone lays claim to his provincial fame: "County Beemaster." And I puzzle over the grave of Ilse and Hilde Neher. Located just to the right of the cemetery entrance, the Neher grave is set with an imposing, waist-high granite stone polished to the high gloss of black patent leather. The grave is always meticulously attended to, the dark earth freshly weeded, a few red geraniums blazing in the shaded light. Like most plots, it contains multiple family names—husband, wife, possibly a sister or mother. At the base of the stone, just inches from the ground, are two inscriptions:

Isle Neher	Hilde Neher
1938–1943	1930–1944

For years I have wondered what tragedy snuffed out these two young lives—at ages five and fourteen—during Dachau's darkest days. The poet Rainer Maria Rilke, who summered in Dachau in the early years of this century, once claimed that how we died, whether quietly or desperately, was the ultimate expression of how we had lived. He saw death as an intimate and deeply personal experience, to be anticipated, like a bottle of finely aged wine. This was, of course, a romantic notion, the musings of a creative spirit pampered in palaces ranging from Paris to Trieste, in the tranquility of the late nineteenth century when people died in bed, the covers tucked to their chins, with family members gathered in silent prayer—not en masse, shaved and stripped, in gas chambers. I used to wonder what kind of poetic lyricism Rilke might have found in the deaths of Ilse and Hilde, these incomplete lives, two innocents who died in an age that had lost all innocence.

One day last spring, while visiting the cemetery, I made a chance encounter before this grave. It was an overcast Thursday morning, and the cemetery was busy with the leisurely traffic of death. An elderly woman stood at the entrance, studying four recent death notices; several people wandered among the graves; deep within the cemetery, washed in the descending green light of the trees, Father Kanzler presided over the burial of an elderly parishioner. I was busy transcribing from stone the history of the Hallmäyrs, a Dachau family that has been proudly—or so the bright gold-leafed inscription would suggest—sacrificing its sons to Teutonic causes for at least three generations. On a large stone triptych imbedded in the cemetery wall, the Hallmäyr family has recorded a century of Hallmäyr heroics. In 1870, Michael Hallmäyr joined the armed Prussian excursion to Paris, survived the victory, and lived to the ripe old age of ninety-five. A generation later, Ludwig and Peter Hallmäyr returned to France to participate in a second round of slaughter. Ludwig, a schoolteacher in Munich, fell on June 14, 1916, at age thirty-two; Michael, a bookbinder by trade and a volunteer in the 5th Battery of the 7th Field Artillery Regiment, perished, probably from wounds, on November 15, 1918, just four days after the armistice that ended the war. He was twenty-six. One war later, Peter Hallmäyr, "son of a master tanner," who earned an Iron Cross Second Class for bravery, fell on the Eastern Front at the age of twenty-eight.

As I studied the valiant and tragic stories of the Hallmäyr boys at war, I heard behind me the rasping and scraping of garden tools. A woman, on her knees before the grave of Ilse and Hilde, worked the soil with a trowel. A rake and tin watering can sat beside her. I watched her meticulously grooming the grave, and when she rose from her labor, I approached her and asked if she could tell me about the two young names inscribed at the bottom of the headstone. She hesitated at first, unsure of why this stranger would ask such a personal question, and then said, "They were my sisters. They were killed while riding their bikes along the wall of the Dachau Concentration Camp."

"At the time, we lived in the Alte Römer Strasse, just down from the camp," the woman told me. "There are five houses there that were used for SS officers and their families." Her father was an SS officer from Allgäu who came to Dachau for training, fell in love with the daughter of the mayor of Augustusfeld, a neighboring town, and settled here. The union produced five children, including Ilse and Hilde. Her father was a stern and imperious man who never expressed a word of regret about his service to National Socialism, and who remained loyal to Hitler until his dying day. He never spoke about his service in the SS; the children never asked.

When her father died, eleven years ago, she realized she knew virtually nothing about his past, only that he had been born in the Allgäu, that he had served for a time at Sachsenhausen, a concentration camp outside Berlin, where she was born, and that he had been captured by the Americans and did not return home until 1947. After his death, she contacted Hans Günter Richardi, who had written several books on Dachau during the Nazi years, and expressed her desire to learn more about her father's past. On Richardi's advice, she traveled to Allgäu to interview people who had known him; she also went to Berlin and toured the Sachsenhausen memorial site with its barbed-wire walls and barracks, to seek traces of his career. She learned that he came from a desperately poor family with a half-dozen siblings, and that the SS offered him the opportunity to escape the poverty of rural mountain life and build a career for himself. He came to Dachau in 1934 and within a year had married. In 1940, he was assigned to Sachsenhausen but several months later found himself back in Dachau. She told me she discovered little about his activities in the SS but did not believe he was actually involved in war crimes. She also related to me the only incident he had ever described from his camp years. While he was escorting a group of *Häftlinge* on a painting assignment outside the camp, several of them bolted and ran. He could not bring himself to shoot them. "Normally you would have been severely disciplined for such a failure, but because my mother was pregnant again he was excused," his daughter recalled. "That is the only thing he ever told us about his time in the SS."

When the family returned to Dachau in 1941, they took up residence in the SS family housing units in the Alte Römer Strasse. The five buildings—sturdy, handsome three-story houses—are still standing and still inhabited. Lace curtains hang in the windows, and there is a swing set in the backyard. The woman recalled that these were idyllic years for the Neher family. Their grandparents lived just down the road, in Augustusfeld. The concentration camp where their father spent his days was just across the street; he could walk to work. They had plenty to eat and enough money to afford small luxuries like a gramophone and bicycles.

One beautiful day in the summer of 1943, Hilde, who was then thirteen, offered to take her five-year-old sister for a bike ride. Her mother had never let Ilse out of the garden, fearing the heavy trucks that lumbered along the road making deliveries to the concentration camp. But this particular day was so beautiful, and the traffic was light. Hilde promised to watch out for her little sister. Standing in the doorway to the house, their mother waved them off and then watched as they headed down the road toward Dachau, Hilde tall and erect on her bike, and little Ilse pedaling like crazy close behind. She waved to them, and called to them to be careful.

Minutes later, after she had gone into the house, the

girls, riding along the perimeter of the white concrete concentration camp wall with its strands of electrified barbed wire overhead, cut in front of the delivery entrance. A truck careened out of the camp at that same instant, hitting both girls broadside. Ilse was killed instantly, and Hilde, thrown from her bicycle, was knocked unconscious. Although she eventually recovered, the following year, while in school, she collapsed and died; the autopsy revealed she had sustained internal injuries to her heart that had never fully healed. The two girls were buried side by side in the family grave.

As we stood there on this gray spring morning in the seclusion of the Dachau cemetery, I imagined the two young girls on their bicycles, their mother at the door, waving to them like any other mother on any other summer day in any other town. I imagined the tinkling laughter of the high-spirited children, their mother's fleeting concern and her rising joy of watching her five-year-old set off on a youthful adventure. And I imagined the moment beyond, with its screeching brakes, the instant of terror, and then the dust and the blood and the twisted metal. One small death on a bright morning in the summer of 1943, a small senseless death at the very edge of the ten-foot concrete wall of the Dachau Concentration Camp.

I looked at the woman, her face saddened by the memory, her hands soiled by the earth of her sisters' grave, and I wasn't quite certain what to say to her. Should I remind her of the thousand other deaths on the other side of that tragic white wall where her sisters fell? Should I remind her of the grief of the thousand other mothers on that same day? Should I invoke the notion of divine justice, of God's revenge on the offspring of a swastika-bound union? Or should I express sorrow for the lost lives of two innocent children who set out on their bikes for an adventure neither would ever remember, for the tragic and senseless loss of young lives? I didn't know what to say because I didn't know myself how I was supposed to feel. I still don't. And so we stood there in silence for a few uncomfortable seconds before she returned to her work, and I headed for Café Teufelhart for a cappuccino.

10

Amid the framed family photographs that clutter a wall in my parents' home—birthdays, weddings, ski trips, beach vacations—is a black-and-white portrait of my mother's family dating from the mid-1930s. In this studio shot, my grandfather stands over his carefully coiffed wife, Midge, and their three children, looking, in his crisp white shirt and three-piece suit, every bit the self-satisfied small-town American businessman that he was.

"The photograph was taken shortly after Dad and your uncle returned from Germany," my mother once told me by way of explanation. "They had seen Hitler at a rally in Berlin, and came home with stories about the remarkable things he was doing for the Germans. Restoring their pride, rebuilding their economy." My mother, who has always turned a blind eye to human failings, insists that her father's infatuation with Adolf Hitler has to be understood in the context of the time. She reminds me that Charles Lindbergh was also an early enthusiast of Adolf Hitler, as was Henry Ford, and that *Time* magazine had declared Hitler its "Man of the Year," before concluding: "This was, of course, before anyone knew anything about his plans for the Jewish people and the death camps."

By all accounts, my grandfather was a man of boundless enthusiasms, who by age thirty-five had transformed himself from Michael Wernitznig, an immigrant boy from rural Austria, into Mike Werner, a small-town American entrepreneur with interests in a frozen-confection factory—Pioneer Ice Cream—a gas station, a car dealership, and numerous parcels of commercial real estate. With his gray suits, his fine cigars, and his breezy confidence, the type engendered by expansive success in a very small place, Mike Werner was the quintessential small-town businessman in America's quintessential small town, Sauk Centre, Minnesota, home to Sinclair Lewis's *Main Street*. Known about town simply as Mike, he was always game for a good joke, a stiff drink, or a hand of poker; on Saturday nights, friends and business associates flocked to his large white house on Birch Street for Victrola dance parties that lasted until the early morning hours. At Christmastime, Mike visited the local schools, handing out bath salts to the teachers and candy canes to the children. When the Irish Catholic church caught fire, he donated money to rebuild the steeple. The Sauk Centre *Eagle* once featured an article extolling Mike Werner's business acumen and civic consciousness.

In 1928, National Ice Cream acquired the frozen-confectionary business my grandfather owned with two partners. He stayed on as general manager of the ice cream division until the summer of 1932, when he decided to give up his position. To celebrate his "retirement," at age forty, he embarked with my uncle, who was then sixteen, on Middle America's version of a "grand tour" of Europe and North Africa, a trip which may in retrospect have been a pivotal experience in Mike Werner's life.

On the evening of February 3, 1933, my grandfather and uncle departed Brooklyn aboard the *Schnelldampfer Columbus*, of the Norddeutscher Lloyd line, and five days later arrived on the island of Madeira. My uncle remembers wandering the shops, tasting the island's distinctive fortified wines, and watching young boys run alongside horsedrawn sledges tossing oiled rags beneath the skids to smooth the ride through the cobblestone streets. The *Columbus* ran a zigzag course through the Mediterranean, from Gibraltar to Casablanca to Malaga to Algiers to Monte Carlo, where my grandfather passed his time gambling, then to Tunis, Sicily, Naples, Malta, and Egypt—there is a photograph of my grandfather perched on a camel before the pyramids—then on to Beirut, Damascus, Istanbul, and finally along the Dalmatian coast, where they eventually disembarked at Trieste. By the spring, they had reached southern Austria. My grandfather spent several weeks looking into the affairs of his farm, which he still owned, visiting relatives, and boasting about the good life in America. He also spent time comforting his sister Johanna, who had just lost her youngest child to the influenza. It was here that my grandfather first heard about the "miracles" that Adolf Hitler was performing in Germany. Having just come to power three months earlier, he had quelled the political chaos that had tormented Germany for nearly two decades. There was order in the streets, and hope in people's hearts. "Leave it to an Austrian to put the German house in order," my grandfather quipped at the time.

Within the month, my grandfather and uncle found themselves in a crush of euphoric Germans on a Munich sidewalk, where, quite by chance, they caught a glimpse of the Führer passing in an open car. "He looked like he does in all the photographs," my uncle recalls. "Except a bit younger." A week later, father and son again stood before Hitler, this time very much by plan at the Tempelhof Airfield outside Berlin, where they joined a million Germans for the famous May Day Rally, the grandest Nazi spectacle to date.

"We were staying at the Hotel Excelsior near the Anhalter Train Station," says my uncle. "I remember waking up and looking out the hotel window, and seeing the *Graf Zeppelin*, the giant dirigible, against the blue morning sky. It was a glorious spring day, what the Germans used to call 'Hitler weather.'" That afternoon, my grandfather and uncle pressed themselves into a crowded tram that clattered out to Tempelhof, where they encountered a sight my uncle has never forgotten, a veritable forest of handheld swastika flags fluttering atop a vast sea of assembled Germans, and, in the distance, the speakers' podium flanked by giant red banners.

Sixty-five years on, my uncle, who possessed a limited command of German, has only vague impressions of the rally itself—the excitement, the crowds, the sensation of repeatedly raising his arm, along with a million others, in the Nazi salute. He relates his memories haltingly and only with a great deal of coaxing. However, newsreel footage and recordings of radio broadcasts vividly capture the spirit and content of that historic day, Tempelhof Field transformed into a luminous temple by a thousand searchlights, Hitler's voice booming into the night, and a sea of euphoric Germans bursting forth in the Nazi party anthem. "Reverent and strong the Horst Wessel Song rises into the eternal evening sky," Joseph Goebbels, the Third Reich image engineer, gushed in his diary later that evening. "The ether waves carry the voice of the million and a half human beings who stand united here in Berlin on the Tempelhof Field, across all of Germany, through cities and towns, and they all join in with us. Here, we are united irresistibly as one. We all belong together, and it is more than an empty phrase to say: We have become a brotherhood."

My uncle, who possesses a keen memory for detail, recalls that they did not get back to their hotel room until quite late that night, and that afterward my grandfather sat at the window enjoying a cigar and listening to the choruses of marching songs and volleys of "Sieg heils" rising from the streets below. But he grows frustratingly vague when it comes to my grandfather's reaction to the May Day Rally; he insists that he cannot recall anything specific, except to say, "At that point, it looked like a pretty good deal." In contrast, my mother vividly remembers her father's unbridled enthusiasm for Hitler, and, in particular, a trove of bright red Nazi regalia, flags, banners, and armbands. On my mother's first day of school, her father stuck a metal swastika pin in the lapel of her coat, patted her on the head, and sent her marching proudly down Main Street U.S.A.

Sixty-five years on, I cannot help but wonder whether the May Day Rally did, as Goebbels claimed it should have, stir my grandfather's Teutonic soul. Did this man who had spent the last two decades fashioning himself into an American citizen, suddenly sense the sap of nationalism rising from his Austrian roots? Did Mike Werner return to the Excelsior Hotel that evening to look in the bathroom mirror and find himself staring into the face of Michael Wernitznig, born of Adolf Hitler's own native soil? I can only speculate on the emotions that moved this forty-year-old entrepreneur from Sauk Centre, Minnesota, that evening in Berlin, but eight years later, with his luck gone bad, my grandfather would be looking to Nazi Germany to realize a dream America was no longer able to fulfill.

11

EMMA WILDENROTTER LOOKED at the Holocaust survivor, an elderly man with a hat, thick glasses, and a cane, and could not believe her good fortune. Having just completed her three months' training as a guide at the concentration camp memorial site, Emma had met several camp survivors, but for the thirty Swiss *Konfirmanden*—recently confirmed Swiss Catholics—she was taking through the camp, it would be the opportunity of a lifetime. She asked the elderly man if he would be willing to answer questions, and when he nodded, she turned to her charges and told them to gather around him. "He is a real survivor," she said. "If you have any questions you should ask him." The young people stared at Martin with near reverence. Those deep, sad eyes had actually seen the horrors the guide had been describing to them; those feet had worn the wooden clogs, that skin had felt the coarse gray-striped uniform, had felt the bite of the winter cold. Only when he began to speak did Emma realize she had made a terrible error.

"It isn't true what this woman is telling you," the man began in his labored German. "It isn't true that this gas chamber was never put into operation. I was an inmate in Dachau. I was here. I saw them lock the doors.

I heard the screams from the gas chamber. I'll bet that woman told you that there, behind Baracke 29, they treated sick inmates. That isn't true. That is the barrack of Dr. Mengele. That is where he performed his experiment with twins." He paused to let the image register, looking slowly into each astonished face. "I saw it with my own eyes."

The old man is confused, Emma thought to herself, then offered respectfully, "I believe that you are speaking about Dr. Rascher. Dr. Mengele was in Auschwitz." The man froze, then turned slowly to Emma and fixed his gaze at her as if moving a large-caliber weapon into position. "You are telling me! You are telling me!" he said brimming with indignation. "What do you know about any of this? Who was in the camp? You or me?" He raised his cane into the air and shook it at her. "You or me? You or me? Who? Tell me! Who?" Astonishment turned to horror as the Swiss *Konfirmanden* looked first at the ancient survivor, then at their tour guide with the Italian accent.

"And that was the end of my tour," Emma says, pausing to brush back her thick brown hair, and reflect on that painful moment two years ago. "I showed them the rest of the camp, the barracks, the watchtower, and took them in to see the twenty-minute film, but I had lost all credibility. For them I was nothing." We sit at Emma's dining room table with cups of espresso, a pot of sugar with a spoon in it, and two Snickers bars at the side. Emma is an attractive Italian woman in her early forties who has lived in Dachau for the past fifteen years. She lives in a new residential development built along the

Alte Münchner Strasse, the old route to Munich, which was regularly traversed by work details from the camp. Her modern house has clean lines, high ceilings, spare white walls, and large picture windows that look out into the garden, and to the Dachau moorlands beyond. Though the house boasts all the trappings of postwar German prosperity, neither Emma nor her husband are German, let alone from Dachau.

"My husband and I moved to Dachau in 1984," says Emma. "We were living in Munich at the time and had just had our first daughter. We wanted to buy our own place, but apartments were expensive in Munich, and besides, we didn't really want to raise a family in the city." Initially, they looked at houses east and south of Munich on the Tegernsee and Starnbergersee but eventually settled on Dachau because of its proximity to Munich—twenty minutes by commuter train—where Emma worked as a speech therapist for handicapped children, and a five-minute car ride to Allach, where her husband, Karl, works in the technology division of MAN, a large corporation involved in developing the *Arianne*, the first European spacecraft. "As soon as I saw Dachau, I said, 'Carletto, that's where I want to live!'" Emma says. By selling part of the family farm she had inherited in Bergamo, Emma and Karl were able to build their dream house. "When my friends back home in Italy heard that I was moving to Dachau," Emma recalls, "they were horrified. They said, 'How can you live in a place called Dachau?'" Personally, says Emma, she had no problem with the idea of owning a home in Dachau. She was used to living with atrocity.

"My father was an Italian soldier and participated in every war Mussolini ever fought with Hitler," Emma tells me. "I spent my entire childhood hearing my father brag about the atrocities he committed. I knew him as a caring father and a loving husband to my mother, but as soon as he got together with his former comrades they would sit around and brag to each other about the horrors they had committed. When they parachuted into the woods in France and came across a fifteen-year-old girl, the entire company took turns raping her. This was my own father. He was a wonderful man, but he was also a killer and a rapist and was proud of it. 'In Greece, we stood up all the Greek partisans and gunned them down,' he used to boast. 'We took Englishmen, stood them up against the wall, and gunned them down, all of them in a row.' He talked about fighting in France, in Greece, in Yugoslavia, and eventually in Russia, where his feet froze. For these exploits, he was richly awarded."

Emma remembers a red plastic box he kept in their home. It was filled with medals, and on special occasions her father would open the box and pin the medals onto his jacket, explaining how many people he had shot for each medal. "He was especially proud of his 'Medaglio de Valore,' which he received for shooting the Greek partisans," says Emma. "As a child I always equated *valor* with *atrocity*. I thought they meant the same thing."

The story of the fifteen-year-old French girl whom her father raped in the woods especially troubled Emma. "Shortly after I turned fifteen myself, I asked my father, 'Do you know what happened to her? Did you kill her? Did you try to find out what happened to her?'

'No, no, we were fighting a war,' he answered. 'We didn't have time for such things.'" She looks me straight in the eye, and I sense she is trying to gauge my own emotional response to the rape of a fifteen-year-old girl in the woods of southern France. "He never expressed a word of regret for what he did, but looking back I believe he was trying to purge himself of these things." Nevertheless, Emma says, her father died convinced that he had fought on "the right side," regretting to the end that Hitler and Mussolini had failed. "Everyone talks about how the Germans ignore their past, that they need to confront it in order to overcome it," Emma says. "With me, it was the opposite. I spent my entire childhood hearing about atrocities. I knew too much. I was poisoned with history."

Shortly after moving to Dachau, Emma became pregnant with their second child. When a psychologist who worked with Emma in Munich learned that she intended to give birth in Dachau, the colleague warned her against the decision. "You can't do that to the child," she said. "The child will be marked for life. If he or she has to show a birth certificate in school, or a passport abroad, there will always be *Dachau*. You can't do such a thing to a child." Another psychologist who worked with Emma and had been living in Dachau since moving from Göttingen two years earlier, told Emma that she still had her Göttingen license plate in order to avoid having the telltale DAH on her car. "It was the first time that I was confronted with how Dachau was perceived from the outside," Emma says. "But I lived in Dachau, and I was not going to pretend I did not." As planned, she gave birth to her second child, also a girl, in Dachau. Two years later, Emma brought a second little *Dachauerin* into this world. (Although all three girls were residents of Dachau, they were in fact by blood and citizenship Italian and Austrian.)

With its good schools and tight-knit community, Dachau was the perfect place to bring up a family. The girls thrived here, joining local sports teams and music clubs, frequenting the ice cream shop near the river, the local movie house in the old town, and the discotheque next to the train station. In the summers, they would visit their relatives in Italy and Austria. Three years ago, while visiting Karl's family in Graz, they took a day excursion to Vienna to look for antique silver boxes at the Dorotheum. Situated on a narrow street in the very center of Vienna, this legendary auction house, which dates back to the time of the Habsburg emperors, is notorious for its lack of parking. Unable to find a parking place near the Dorotheum, Emma and Karl decided to drop the girls off and look for a place to leave the car. As the girls stepped out of the car, an elderly man suddenly came running down the street toward them, shaking his fists and screaming, "Ihr Judenvergaser! Ihr vergast die Juden!" Stunned by the attack, the girls fled into the Dorotheum and the man continued down the street, shaking his fists. The incident was quickly forgotten and the family enjoyed a pleasant day in Vienna. However, that evening back in Graz, Emma's younger daughter asked her mother, "What did that man say to us? Was he drunk?" Emma told her that he had called them a *Judenvergaser* and then found herself explaining to her children, as delicately as she could, what it meant to "gas a Jew," and how this was related to their hometown. When Emma finished, her youngest daughter looked at her and asked, with painful sincerity, "Mama, bin ich ein Judenvergaser?" The following summer, while they were visiting Emma's family in Bergamo, all four tires of their car were slashed.

"By nature, I am not a melancholy person," Emma says when she has finished telling me these stories. "I love life. I love having fun. I go bowling in Munich with my girlfriends. I like to go to Prague for a weekend, or to Italy on vacation. I have a wonderful home. My life here in Dachau is beautiful, but when I am confronted with these realities outside the town, I see that it's true, you cannot live a normal life in Dachau."

On the day we meet, Emma is preparing to take a unit of fifty Bundeswehr—German army—recruits on a tour of the former concentration camp. Following recent revelations of rightist-extremist tendencies within the ranks of their armed forces, the German high command has mandated a tour of a former concentration camp for all *Bundeswehrler* at some point during their eighteen months of military service. Increasingly, Emma has specialized in sensitizing German soldiers to the horrors of the Holocaust, and has helped design a special five-hour program, two hours longer than the standard tour for most groups. "Normally, if you tell young people about the *Appellplatz* and how the *Häftlinge* had to assemble there in the middle of winter at five o'clock every morning, or about how they would be severely punished if anything was out of order in the barracks, they say, 'Oh my God, how horrible,' " Emma observes. "But say that to a military recruit, and he just looks at you and says, 'So what? We go through that every day. Why are these people considered such martyrs and we are just *Bundeswehrler?* I was locked up for three days just because my locker was not in order.' " Some recruits have just returned from a tour of duty in Bosnia and say they don't need any lessons in atrocity. Instead of presenting the standard-issue Holocaust horrors, Emma says she attempts to touch the soldiers' *Gewissen*—their conscience.

To this end, she convenes a group discussion following the tour of the camp in which she attempts to get the recruits to open up about their feelings about the Holocaust. Because commanding officers are required to report any expression of anti-Semitic or rightist-extremist sentiment in their ranks, Emma generally asks the officers to excuse themselves from the discussions. She then seats the soldiers in a circle on the floor and hands each of them a pack of eight cards, each card a different color, each with a different question: *Were the SS men in the concentration camps beasts, or is there something of an SS man in each of us? What did people know about the concentration camps, and what did they do with this knowledge? Where was God in the concentration camps? Where is God today when we need him?* Each soldier selects the question that has the most meaning for him, places it on top, and then tosses his pack into the center of the circle.

According to Emma, almost everyone chooses either the blue or the pink card:

Are we still guilty today for what happened back then? Not only Germans have committed horrific crimes—why do people ignore the crimes of others?

Emma then asks each soldier in turn to respond to the questions. "They are uncertain at first and give careful, safe answers," says Emma. "But then one soldier will ask why no one mourns for the half-million German soldiers who died at Stalingrad, and another will ask why the Americans were never tried for the atrocities they committed in Vietnam." As opinions accumulate, the emotions intensify. Emma says that she hears emotions ranging from vicious rightist-extremist rhetoric to moving expressions of guilt and remorse. After an hour of intense, often heated debate, she closes the discussion by distributing a letter from 1943 written by a German farm boy who refused to join the SS.

My dear parents, I must give you the sad news that I have been sentenced to death. I and Gustav G. refused to join the SS and have been sentenced to die. You wrote me that I should under no circumstances join the SS. My comrade Gustav G. and I have therefore refused to sign. Both of us would rather die than stain our conscience with such atrocities. I know what the SS men have to do. Oh, dear parents, as difficult as all this may be, please forgive me. If I have offended you, please forgive me and pray for me. If I had died in battle and had a bad conscience, that would also be sad for you. There will be many more parents who will lose their children. SS men die as well. I thank you for everything you have done for me since my childhood. Your son.

There is a grim stillness in the room as the soldiers read the letter. This is followed by a muted discussion. "By the time they leave the room, they are no longer thirty men in uniform," Emma says. "They are thirty individuals, each with their own lives, their own thoughts, their own fates. Just like the Holocaust survivors."

12

"ME LLAMO MARTIN ZAIDENSTADT," Martin says to the couple who reply to his salutation with blank stares. "Ja znam Martina Zaidenstadta," Martin repeats, in Polish. Still no response. With a glance at the shoes or the jacket or even the gestures or gait, Martin is generally able to decipher a visitor's provenance. Three years and thousands of encounters have honed his detective instincts. But this middle-aged couple, with their curious mixture of fashionable shoes, leather jackets, and pallid Central European complexions, baffles him. When Russian brings no response, he says, "Ich heiße Martin Zaidenstadt." Recognition registers on their faces; Martin knows they must be "Ossies," residents of the former East Germany whose stylish trappings cannot fully obscure the traces of a lifetime spent eating red cabbage and inhaling anthracite coal. Continuing in his heavily accented German, Martin performs his standard Holocaust details and memories, then, as an encore, adds, "I am eighty-seven years old. Becoming old man." Pointing to his right eye, he observes, "This eye no longer works." He then tugs at his left ear. "This ear doesn't work." After rapping his right calf with his cane—"This leg doesn't work"—he opens his mouth in a horselike grin that exposes two rows of flawless white dentures. Then his teeth begin to clatter. The two Ossies watch in bewildered astonishment as Martin's dentures come loose from his gums and gradually work themselves forward until they protrude grotesquely beyond his lips, clapping wildly like a skeleton jaw in a grade-B horror film.

It is two o'clock on a Sunday afternoon and Martin has been greeting a steady stream of camp visitors since the memorial site opened at nine A.M. With the exception of a brief break to eat his banana and packet of crackers, he has been on his feet, sometimes leaning heavily on his cane, before the crematorium.

Recently, he has begun to show people the tattered *New York Times* article about him that he keeps folded in his wallet. It has a photograph of Martin outside the crematorium and bears the headline HOLOCAUST SURVIVOR KEEPS LONELY VIGIL. It appeared in October 1997 and was written by Alan Cowell. "He sent me a check for twenty dollars, but it cost so much to cash the check that I sent it back to him and told him to send me cash," Martin tells me, then adds with a smile: "He sent me a twenty-dollar bill."

On this particular afternoon, Martin has spoken to well over forty people, and sold, by my count, at least a dozen cards. At one point, a group of thirty or so Israeli youths cross the bridge from the main camp and enter the cloistered setting of the crematoria buildings. The men all wear yarmulkes; several have large Israeli flags draped down their backs. One man in his mid-twenties is wearing a tallith, the fringed prayer shawl with bands of black and blue worn by Orthodox Jews at prayer and on solemn occasions.

"Why you wear a tallith here?" Martin asks with a sharp edge to his voice. "Tallith is only for the temple. Synagogue. Why you wear tallith here?" Martin has planted himself before the man like a wall. The young man is large, with closely cut dark hair. He glares defiantly at Martin.

"Are you a Jew?" he asks.

"You are not supposed to wear tallith here," Martin repeats. "Tallith is only for holy place."

"I wear this here because it is a holy place."

Martin stares fiercely into his eyes. His face darkens, he raises his cane from the ground, and suddenly erupts in a terrifying rage. "This is not a holy place," he roars. "This is a place of death, a place of murder, a place of horror. This is not a holy place. This is no place for tallith."

The man looks stunned by the outburst, but quickly recovers and repeats, "Are you Jewish?"

With his face still clouded with rage, Martin begins to recite the Kaddish, then he recites another Hebrew prayer, and another, and another. The Israelis gather around him and watch him with astonishment. As he chants, his expression softens, a look of peace returns to his face. When he finishes, he turns to the young man wearing the tallith and says, "I live in Dachau. I come here every day. Every day for fifty years. My name is Mordechai, Mordechai Zaidenstadt."

"Were you born in Poland?" the man with the tallith asks.

"All my family come from Poland."

"My family came from Poland. From Łomza," the Israeli says.

"Łomza?" says Martin with surprise. "What is the mother's name?"

"Kirchmann."

"Łomza, Nowgrod, Stettin, Marburg, Grunberg," Martin begins to chant, then stops abruptly, looks the Israeli in the eye, and says, "I live in Dachau. I come every day. I stay in Israel before you are baby."

"Do you have a wife?" the Israeli asks. "Where is your wife?"

"Here in Dachau, alive," Martin says, then switches to German. "Meine Familie ist alle ermordet worden"— My entire family was murdered. "I speak Spanish. You speak Spanish?"

"No, I speak Hebrew and English."

The conversation rambles, then dissipates. As the group departs, Martin begins to sing in Hebrew. It is a simple, cheerful melody, like a children's song. The Israelis turn and laugh. Martin smiles, and continues to sing to himself until the words and melody trail off and vanish. An American couple, who have been watching the exchange with the Israelis, approach.

"You were here on the day the camp was liberated?" the man asks.

Martin stares at them for a moment with irritated distraction. "Ich war hier am Tag der Befreiung?" he repeats the question in German before answering, "Ja, ich war hier am Tag der Befreiung."

"Forty-second Division, right?"

"Zweiundvierzigste Division," Martin repeats, then he continues to talk, in German, about the fact that no one ever escaped from Dachau, looking to me to provide translation. There were escapes from Mauthausen and Sachsenhausen and Bergen-Belsen, but never a single successful escape from Dachau. *Häftlinge* tried to escape, but they were either gunned down by the guards or tripped up on the electrified barbed wire. Dachau was that well defended. When the 42nd Division arrived and saw the horrifying conditions in the camp, they lined the camp guards up against a wall and executed them all on the spot. "Peng, peng, peng!" Martin concludes. "Alle ermordet auf der Stelle ohne Prozeß." Everyone murdered on the spot without a trial. He stares at them to see their reaction, his jaw set like a boxer preparing for a fight. When he has finished and the couple have left, I ask him why he had not spoken English. "Today, I don't speak English," he continues in German. "I speak Polish. I speak Spanish. I speak German. No English today."

The encounter with the Israelis has inspired a wellspring of Hebrew songs. Martin sings bits and pieces of cheerful ditties, smiling to himself, interrupting them to chat with a group of Japanese tourists who videotape him in the gas chamber, a young woman from Madrid with whom he engages in an extended exchange in Spanish, a large number of Americans, and a German hippie—ponytail, sandals, and backpack—who arrives at the cremerory compound on a bicycle. He tells Martin that he is biking to every former concentration camp in Germany, collecting a leaf, a bit of grass or some soil or stones. He tells Martin about his travels, barely registering Martin's own story, then hops on his bike and rides from the camp. When one man asks if it hurt to have a number tattooed on his arm, Martin replies, "No number on wrist. Prisoner of war don't need number." He pulls up his right sleeve, then his left sleeve, and extends both arms outward as evidence. His aged skin is wrinkled and white, not blemished by the faded numbers—often blurred to indistinctness—I have seen on the arms of so many Holocaust survivors. As the man walks away, Martin stares at his wrists for a long moment, as if looking for a trace of a number himself, then rolls down his sleeves. He again takes up a Hebrew song, and as he loses the words and melody, he mutters to himself, "Tallith is only for the synagogue, not here. When the rabbi leaves the synagogue he removes tallith. And they didn't need to bring the flags either. That has nothing to do with what happened here."

13

WHEN MARTIN ZAIDENSTADT pulled the gun on me in his office, I think he was trying to make a point about dying in Dachau. Were he to have pulled the trigger, and were he to have hit his target, there would have been telephone calls, police cars, an ambulance, an emergency room visit at the Dachau County Hospital, or, at the very least, a respectable funeral at the Denk Funeral Home.

It wasn't always that way in Dachau. There was a time when death was as close as a mistaken step or a glance cast in the wrong direction. In those days, death hovered like the hawk circling the unplowed field, waiting to lunge in an instant and pluck a life, a mouse, a mole, a scurrying rabbit, from the earth. A momentary flutter and scuffle, a death, and then the return of the world to its normal order. Not unlike that beautiful spring morning in 1943 or 1944, Martin cannot remember which, when death claimed the Polish inmate Jerzy Czermanski.

Martin has told me countless stories about deaths that were as everyday as they were senseless. Some, I am certain, are based on personal experience, and others, I suspect, have been gleaned from hearsay or films or books, and have, in the course of time, gradually come to share a common reality in Martin's memory. He remembers seeing Russian prisoners-of-war marched from the camp to the nearby SS gun range at Hebertshausen where they were placed on a stage in a concrete amphitheater and used for target practice; he has heard the screams of children gassed in the camp ovens, of children torn apart by camp dogs, of two Polish Jews near Karlsfeld who were hanged by the neck in front of their fellow inmates, and of his fellow inmate, Jerzy Czermanski, who was killed for casting a glance at three local maidens strolling down the road between Dachau and Etzenhausen.

It is early morning, and the dawn has sliced open the night, spilling the first light across the Dachau moors. Martin and Jerzy, along with five thousand other Dachau *Häftlinge*, have assembled on the *Appellplatz* for the morning roll call and the assignment to the work details. For the last week, they have been marched each morning to the surrounding fields, where they are put to work breaking the winter-packed fields for the spring planting. Martin does not care for the hard labor in the fields, with its bending and hacking, but Jerzy relishes the work. Having grown up on a small farm outside Łomza, he welcomes the strain in his back and the smell of the soil. Beyond the confines of the camp, and with a hoe in his hands as he slices into the rich loam, he can imagine himself lifting and hacking in his family's fields. He is fortunate that the Germans don't trust the Poles with masonry or handiwork—that is work for Italians and Frenchmen and their own Teutonic brothers—and instead send them to the fields, like draft animals.

As the sun is clearing the horizon, fifteen Polish *Häftlinge*, including Martin and Jerzy, are marched through the Jourhaus Gate, through the SS compound, then beyond the camp perimeter into the brilliant spring countryside east of Dachau toward Etzenhausen. The morning light casts the gentle green foliage of the distant woods in gold. Overhead, the morning haze is drawing back to reveal a flawless blue sky. It promises to be a magnificent spring day.

Within half an hour, the work commando is scattered across a field, and pairs of SS guards are standing about with their guns shouldered. Most are smoking cigarettes. As Martin hacks at the packed soil, he overhears a guard with a harelip complaining about the local girls, how they look first at the insignia to see the rank before they decide how friendly they should be, and with so many officers here for training, it is virtually impossible for an SS man below officer's rank to have a chance.

"If you don't like it, get promoted," the other guard says, lighting a fresh cigarette. As their conversation turns to their upcoming leave, three Dachau girls dressed in local garb come walking up the road, wicker baskets under their arms. Two are somewhat heavyset with dark hair, the third is slender and attractive with thick brunette hair. The two men follow the girls with their eyes, until the guard with the harelip catches a glimpse of Jerzy looking at them as well, and yells, "Was schaust du denn an?"

The girls glance in their direction. The guard looks at them, then at Jerzy, and barks again, "Was schaust du denn an?"

"Keep working," Martin whispers to Jerzy, staring down at the ground and working his hoe like mad. A minute later, Martin and Jerzy find themselves hustled to the side of the road, the guard with the harelip screaming in their faces, "Was schaut ihr denn an? Versteht ihr mich? Versteht ihr mich?" and glancing furtively toward the three girls along the road. Martin knows thing are going very wrong now. He is standing straight, as straight as he can, trying to make things right. The angry guard is no longer distinguishing between them. He screams at Martin and slaps him on the side of the face. Martin's cheek stings but he stands erect, staring straight ahead. The guard slaps him again, then, wheels around and strikes Jerzy with the back of his hand, grazing the side of his head and sending his cap flying into the ditch.

"Herbert, they're gone," the other guard says. "They're not looking."

But Herbert doesn't care. He looks at Jerzy, at the terror in his face, and the cap—*Mütze*—lying in the ditch.

"Mütze!" he screams.

But Jerzy is frozen with terror. A cap on the ground. Everyone knows what that means. It lies there in the ditch, gray-striped, like a lifeless rodent, and all four men know what that means. The others in the field do not look up.

"Mütze!" Herbert screams again.

But Jerzy does not budge. He knows what it means to break rank. He knows what it means to head for the side of the road. A bullet in the back. A bullet in the back for fleeing. And so he stands there with his fists clenched and his eyes closed and the raging SS man screaming, "Mütze! Mütze! Mütze!" And then the sidearm cracks, Jerzy trembles, exhales audibly, like a spurt of air released from a tire, and drops to the ground. Herbert glances at the girls, who are now farther down the road to Dachau. They do not even glance back.

That night in his wooden bunk, Martin still feels the weight of his comrade, whom he and another *Häftling* had dragged back to the camp and left beside the gate to be hauled away to the crematorium. He still feels the terror that gripped him as the gun was drawn, as the cold steel pressed against his skull and was then withdrawn. His face still smarts from the blow. As he lies there, he feels water on his hands and realizes he is crying. It has been a long time since he has cried. Since his sister died twelve years ago. Martin cries long and deep, and as he sobs he is surprised to find himself weeping not for his comrade but for himself. He came so close to dying. He is so fortunate to be alive.

14

I CANNOT FIND MARTIN ZAIDENSTADT. I run my finger carefully down the list of names, Zaial, Zaic, Zaice, Zaidl, Zaimel. There is no Martin Zaidenstadt. I read through the list of names again, then return to the top of the page, take an index card, and go through the list of names again, the card guiding my eyes, line by line, name by name, until I am absolutely certain I have not missed Martin's name. Zaidenstadt should appear between Vladimir Zaic and Hans Zaidl. He is not there. I glance through the pages before and after to make certain he was not accidentally out of place, but there is no trace of Martin Zaidenstadt.

I am seated in the archives of the concentration camp memorial site, which is housed in the camp's former laundry rooms. It is a clean, brightly lit space with white walls, tile floors, linoleum tables, fluorescent lights, an appropriately clinical place for Holocaust scholars to dissect the piles of documents left behind by the Third Reich, to perform their autopsies on this fallen *corpus germanicus*. I am here to find Martin Zaidenstadt in the camp registry, thirty or so binders with nearly two hundred thousand names in alphabetical order that were compiled from camp records immediately after the war. But Martin is not among them.

As a former academic familiar with the idiosyncrasies of archival work, I decide to consult with Barbara Distel, the memorial site's highly competent director who has helped me in the past with similar searches. She is on vacation, I am told, but her deputy is more than happy to assist me. When I tell her that I am seeking to confirm the identity of a former camp inmate and that my initial searches have brought nothing, she informs me that the camp records are indeed incomplete, especially for the early years. The camp had an estimated 220,000 inmates during its twelve-year history, and the archives contain only 180,000 names. When I mention that the inmate I am seeking was a prisoner of war, she says he would certainly be registered. When I mention that the inmate's name is Martin Zaidenstadt, she gives me a knowing look and says, "We know him well. He is definitely in the registry."

She takes me into a brightly illuminated room behind the archive library and shows me the original bound typescript version of the inmate registry. She pulls out a bound volume marked *XYZ*, and opens it to the page where Martin's name should be. Like me, she quickly comes to the names Vladimir Zaic and Hans Zaidl.

Zaic   *Poznań, 12.3.42 Sch.h. R.K. 36-85-52*
     Vladimir   *6.11.43. n. Sachsenh. 21.6.44 z.n. D. gest. 13.3.45*

Zaidl   *Berlin, 6.7.43.J. 89-65-36.*   *Pflichtarbeit.*
     Hans   *gest. 4.6.44 Körperschw.*

As Distel's deputy views the names, instinctively she begins to decipher the concentration camp shorthand. "Vladimir Zaic. He was arrested in Poznań on March 12, 1942. He was Roman Catholic. The 'Sch.h.' is shorthand for *Schutzhäftling*," she explains—protective custody. "He was transferred to Sachsenhausen on November 6, 1943, and then returned to Dachau the following June. He died in March 1945." She pauses, then begins to narrate Hans Zaidl, a Jew who was arrested in Berlin on July 6, 1943, and immediately brought to Dachau, where he was placed on a labor detail. He spent the entire time in the camp until his death in June 1944. According to the record he died of *Körperschwäche*—body weakness—the combined rigors of hunger, labor, and disease.

When I point to the entry above Zaic, for which there is only a name, a registration number, and a large blank followed by the date 17.2.45, she observes that it is strange that there is no other information, since the low registration number suggests that he was in the camp for a long time. She also notes that he died two months before the camp was liberated. Probably from disease. Another entry is marked "Rk.n.e."—*Rückkehr nicht erwunscht*—return not desired—a camp euphemism for an inmate dispatched to an extermination facility. She falls silent, then stares at the table. "Just a lot of numbers and letters, but so much suffering," she murmurs. "It is almost unbearable."

Distel's assistant finds it strange that Martin Zaidenstadt is not in the registry. She knows his case well, and is certain they have found him in the camp records previously. As I had done with the public documents in the other room, she scans adjacent pages, then checks alternate spellings for his name: Zeidenstadt, Seidenstadt, Saidenstadt, Saitenstadt. When I suggest that Martin may have been entered under his Polish name, she finds a Polish-German dictionary and looks up the Polish for *Seide*, silk: *Wabno*. We return to the registry, but again the search yields nothing. She pauses for a moment, visibly perplexed, then calls another colleague and asks him to look in a special file they keep on notable camp inmates. The colleague goes over to a large filing cabinet, pulls open the drawer, and returns to us a few minutes later empty-handed. When I begin to ask her about Martin's presence in the camp, she grows nervous, tells me that she cannot really comment on him, and suggests I come back after Barbara Distel returns from vacation.

15

As in much of Europe, August is a quiet time in Dachau. Once the annual Volksfest has concluded, and the crowds who visit the town to enjoy the "cheapest beer in Bavaria" have dispersed, the town slips quietly into its traditional late-summer doldrums. While Dachau residents pass idle hours at the streetside tables outside Café Teufelhart or Hotel Zieglerbräu, or relax on the sunsplashed terrace of the Dachau Schloss looking out over the manicured garden and the dramatic north face of the Alps a hundred kilometers to the south, a mile to the west throngs of visitors crowd the concentration camp memorial site. Only occasionally does an American, Polish, or Japanese tourist stray into the old town, walking uneasily through the cobblestone streets, then vanishing.

August wasn't always like this in Dachau. In another era, the summer streets teemed with painters and poets from across Europe. The trains from Munich rolled into the Dachau train station, unloading gay parties of day visitors who trooped through town and into the countryside to watch artists, some from as far away as Russia, Sweden, and America, at work on Dachau's legendary moors and meadows.

A distinguished poet who visited the artists' commu-

nity in the last decade of the previous century observed
that the Dachau moors possessed a distinctive charm as
enchanting as the blue-eyed glance, as alluring as the
flaxen hair of the local maidens. He spoke of a harmo-
nious but tragic beauty, claiming that in the stillness of
the morning hours, in that mystical moment just before
daybreak, when night breathes its final sigh, you could
hear across the darkened moorlands the ancient lament
of Teutonic women who wept and bled to the secret
rhythms of the tugging lunar cycle. They wailed beneath the jaundiced moon for fallen lovers and stillborn
infants, for ancient drives and secret needs, like portents
of future tragedy. There was something, he believed,
that was distinctively feminine, even sensuous, about
Dachau's surrounding hills and moorlands. According to
Otto Fuchs, there still is.

"If you look at the curves of the female form, you will
see the Dachau landscape, the same contours, the same
simple lines of the horizon, a gentle series of curved
lines in dialogue with one another," Fuchs tells me.
"Watch." With practiced hand, he draws a curved hori-
zontal line, then another, and another, and as the pencil
scrapes and scratches across the paper, the gentle hills of
the Dachau countryside emerge from the paper, the
rolling landscape east and north of town, beyond the
Leitenberg, where the corpses of the concentration
camp dead are buried, off toward the hamlets of
Webling, Etzenhausen, and Prittlbach.

Fuchs pauses to study his handiwork. "Now watch."
He draws the same gently curved line, then another, like
two elegant parentheses, one slightly higher than the

other. He draws another set above the first, then another and another and another, and as the artist's hand plies its trade, a reclining female figure begins to appear, first a calf, then a thigh, then two legs and the gentle curve of the hips and then full, ample breasts, then the arms, and finally her head, cocked slightly to the left.

"You see, nothing but the same two lines repeated over and over and over again," Fuchs says with a smile. "That is the genius of the female form." A pause—"and the Dachau landscape." Though Fuchs has been drawing and painting for nearly seventy years, he seems truly enchanted by the power of a few penciled lines to evoke such palpable reality.

We are seated in Fuchs's spacious apartment that also serves as his studio. The walls are hung floor to ceiling with Fuchs's paintings, some landscapes, some portraits, mostly female nudes. At ninety-two years, Otto Fuchs is the *éminence grise* among Dachau artists, the town's last link to a time when a gentler spirit inhabited this breast and slope of German soil.

Otto Fuchs first came to Dachau in the spring of 1938 when, as an aspiring young artist, he walked from Essen to Munich in search of an inspiring setting. "I wandered through the countryside around Munich for several weeks, pitching my tent near various towns," he recalls. Late one night, while walking along a dirt road west of Schleißheim, Fuchs caught sight of the Dachau Schloss, perched high on a hill and bathed in moonlight. He knew he had found his home. Except for a four-year tour of duty in the German army, spent mostly on the Eastern front as one of a handful of *Kriegsmaler*—war painters—Fuchs has lived his life in Dachau, where he has left an indelible mark on the town's artistic life. His work hangs in the town hall, in the local art museum, in numerous shops, and on the walls of countless Dachau households. According to Fuchs, known in town as "Akt-Fuchs" for his singular dedication to the female form, "no small number" of Dachau residents have over the years discreetly brought their wives to him for a "portrait." "You never really know what a woman looks like until you get her clothes off," observes Fuchs, who has been surprised by many of Dachau's *Hausfrauen*. "You see these women on the street or in a shop in town and they look rather plain, but with their clothes off they really can look quite attractive." At the same time, he says, women who appear enticing when fully clothed can lose much of their charm in the buff. Based on the array of female nudes adorning his walls, it is clear that Fuchs cultivates the Rubensian penchant for full-fleshed women. Though these discreet sittings have diminished in recent years, Fuchs continues to wonder what these couples, most of whom have children, actually do with the paintings when they get them home. "It isn't really the kind of thing you hang in the dining room and invite the neighbors to see," Fuchs says and with a wry smile adds, "Then again, maybe it is."

In August 1984, Otto Fuchs was catapulted to national prominence when one of his nudes, *Asian Aphrodite*, became the centerpiece for a fierce debate on art, pornography, religion, and freedom of expression, not the sorts of things people usually talk about in Dachau. That summer, Fuchs was asked to contribute several works of art for an exhibition of local artists intended to reestablish Dachau's reputation as a leading center of artistic activity. The idea was the brainchild of the town's mayor, Lorenz Reitmeier, who, arguing that twelve years of National Socialist terror could not be allowed to eradicate twelve hundred years of a proud cultural heritage, had set out on a quixotic crusade to fight history with art. As part of his campaign to transform Dachau from *KZ-Stadt* to *Kunststadt*, from the hearth of horror to the city of art, Reitmeier constructed a state-of-the-art gallery, subsidized artists' ateliers, and undertook an ambitious acquisition campaign, rifling galleries and auction houses across Europe in search of artwork from *fin-de-siècle* Dachau.

The crowning achievement of this Reitmeier Renaissance was the renovation of the Dachau Schloss, the eighteenth-century rococo structure whose library, local lore holds, served Carl Spitzweg as the model for his classic Biedermeier painting *The Bookworm*. To mark the completion of the Schloss renovation, Reitmeier planned a major exhibition that involved forty of Dachau's best painters, sculptors, and graphic artists. Among their number, of course, was Otto Fuchs, who contributed five canvases, including his *Asian Aphrodite*. Borrowing generously from "heathen iconography"—a breast here, a penis there—Fuchs fashioned a stylized portrait of a woman, naked from the waist up, her left hand cupping her left breast from below, and her right hand extended with open palm skyward, serving as a

platform for three erect penises braided into an evoca-
tive symbol of fertility. Despite the "heathen" body
parts, the face of his Aphrodite radiated the classic dead-
pan innocence of an early Christian-era Madonna. The
aura around her head looked deceptively—shall we say
dangerously?—similar to a halo.

On the day the exhibition opened, Fuchs received a
telephone call from a friend informing him that Hans
Hartl, a Dachau lawyer who was running for a seat
on the Town Council, had been "deeply offended" by
Fuchs's rendering of the Virgin Mary. Fuchs responded
that the painting depicted "neither a virgin nor a Mary."
It was, as the title suggested, an Asian Aphrodite. A day
later, Fuchs opened the *Dachauer Nachrichten*, the conservative local daily, to see a picture of his *Aphrodite*
beside an editorial by Hans Hartl that bore the headline
TASTELESS AND OFFENSIVE.

Venting the full measure of small-town self-
righteousness that only an election year can produce,
Hartl excoriated Fuchs and his painting. The Hartl
harangue, in turn, unleashed a torrent of readers' letters
that tore through the editorial pages of the local newspapers, and was echoed in heated debates throughout
town. As cries rose that the painting be burned, and
Fuchs harbored serious concern that it might fall to the
knife of a moral zealot, local artists and journalists rallied around Fuchs and his *Aphrodite*, insisting on artistic
freedom, and invoking sinister memories of "book
burnings" and the "blackest epoch of the German past."
By week's end, the furor had echoed beyond Dachau's
cobblestoned ways, and was reverberating in the sacro-

sanct chambers of the Catholic Archdiocese of Munich, which publicly castigated Reitmeier and demanded that he remove this *"barbusige Madonna,"* bare-breasted Madonna, immediately. Pious as he might be, Reitmeier stood by the cause of artistic freedom, insisting that the Fuchs painting remain on the palace wall.

However, on Saturday morning, an indignant town official, accompanied by the local priest, marched into the exhibition, removed the *objet d'horreur,* and unceremoniously delivered it at the doorstep of a local architect who had purchased the offending work. As word spread that the Fuchs painting had been removed, an angered group of artists stormed the Dachau Schloss, intent on withdrawing their works in protest. Seeking to salvage the inaugural exhibition, and with it Dachau's reputation as a *Kunststadt,* Reitmeier dashed up the cobblestone path leading from the old town to the Schloss, where he vainly pleaded with the artists not to remove their work.

Today, Fuchs reflects on the scandal over the bare-breasted Madonna with a mixture of pride, that his artwork could have unleashed such powerful emotions, and bewilderment, that Lorenz Reitmeier could actually believe that an art exhibition could either help or harm Dachau's international reputation. "I know what Dachau means to me, and I love this city," Fuchs says. "But I also know what the rest of the world thinks of this place, and that regardless of what I paint or don't paint, for the rest of the world Dachau will always remain Dachau."

16

FOR ALL THE MILLIONS of dollars that have gone into renovating Dachau's rococo Schloss, the cheerful handsome building simply cannot compete with a less ornate but infinitely more compelling Dachau tourist attraction—the *Brausebad*, or shower, a concrete chamber with two iron doors and an ominously low ceiling fitted with sixteen funnel-shaped "shower heads." Situated in Baracke X in the northeast corner of the former concentration camp, this tight, dimly lit space attracts as many as a million visitors annually. It is a still and chilling place. The screams that Martin once heard, or still hears, are not audible to those who enter; in the oppressive silence of the gas chamber you hear only the hard, tight breathing of the visitors who pause for a moment to try and imagine the unthinkable as they stare at the sign in the corner that, in German, English, French, Italian, and Russian—all languages of Martin—reads:

GASKAMMER
getarnt als "Brausebad"
—war nicht in Betrieb

GAS CHAMBER
disguised as a "shower room"
—never used as a gas chamber

CHAMBRE À GAZ
"chambre de douche" camouflée
—ne fuit jamais utilisée

CAMERA A GAS
camuffata da "bagno a doccia"
—non fu messa in funziore

Камера для газа
маскированная как "душ"
-не бЫл в действии

This multilingual stanza of historic truth has become something of a mantra for the residents of Dachau. "Die Gaskammer wurde nie benutzt," Lorenz Reitmeier has told me over coffee at the Dachau Schloss. "Die Gaskammer wurde nie benutzt," Heinrich Rauffer has told me while hanging the latest Burberrys fashion in his shop window. "Die Gaskammer wurde nie benutzt." I have been told by Bruno Schachtner and Emma Wildenrotter and Barbara Distel and just about everyone else with whom I have spoken in town. They tell you this over hot chocolate at Café Teufelhart, or sitting over a beer in front of Hotel Zieglerbräu, or standing in the Neue Galerie, or over Wienerschnitzel and potatoes at their dining room table. It is important to Dachauers that you know that, despite the presence of that bedroom-size chamber in Baracke X, Zyklon B was never employed for homicidal purposes in Dachau. In fact, Hans Junker, a former Dachau mayor, once argued that since the damn thing had never been used it should have been torn down, because it gave visitors the wrong impression.

"Unfortunately, most people fail to make one important distinction when it comes to Baracke X," observes Hans Günter Richardi, "and that is: on the one hand there is the gas chamber, and on the other the crematorium. Most people think they are the same thing." It frustrates Richardi that people don't understand that the gas chamber, as its name suggests, is used for administering poison gas, whereas the crematorium is used for incinerating human remains. "Even during tours, I have to constantly make clear to people that even though the gas chamber was not used, the crematorium was necessary just to keep pace with the large number of deaths." Richardi uses the term *Todesernte*—death harvest.

It is safe to say that Hans Günter Richardi, author of several books on Dachau and founder of an organization devoted to exploring local history, knows more about the former concentration camp than just about anyone else in town, more than most of us would need to know or even want to know. He can tell you that the new crematorium, which was completed in 1943, was known first as Der Bunker, then as X Baracke, and finally as Baracke X. He can also tell you how long it took to construct Baracke X, the names of those involved in its construction, the exact day the ovens were first fired up, approximately how many bodies were incinerated, and the month—November 1944—the ovens finally idled because of a shortage of coke.

By the time the Rainbow Division liberated the camp, in 1945, Richardi notes, the unburned corpses were piled to the ceiling. The American soldiers were so appalled by what they saw that they lined the camp's three hundred SS guards up against a wall and summarily executed them. Richardi shows me a series of black-and-white photographs of American GIs with rifles slung at their sides, standing before piles of corpses in German uniforms along a wall that is pocked with bullet-holes. "Unfortunately, most of these camp guards were in fact Romanian kids who had only recently been pressed into SS service and installed in the camp," Richardi tells me; "the regular SS guards had fled a few weeks before."

A dark-haired man in his late forties, Richardi delivers his facts and statistics with unbridled passion. He leaps up and shuffles through boxes for documents, he reads from books and photocopies, and when he feels he has delivered enough information to make his point, he falls silent and stares at you through his thick, horn-rimmed glasses, like an artillery gunner waiting for the dust to clear to see what effect his barrage has had. But for all his boxes and photographs, Richardi cannot provide me with a single document refuting Martin Zaidenstadt's assertion that the gas chamber was indeed *im Betrieb*, that he knew the people who slammed the doors, that he heard the victims' screams. He can only counter Holocaust survivor testimony with Holocaust survivor testimony. "I have interviewed a Baukapo"—

the inmate responsible for building and operating Baracke X—"and he assured me that the gas chamber was never put into operation." Richardi also says he has photocopies of a number of letters by former camp inmates claiming that the gas chamber was never used.

Why, I wondered, would someone have built such an elaborate contraption—with all its attendant pipes, valves, vents, and rubber seals—only to leave it idle, especially amid this panoply of death with its gallows, its execution wall, and, down a wooded path behind Baracke X, a slight depression in the earth that served as a *Blutrinne*—a blood ditch—where SS guards administered the ritual *Genickschuss*—a single bullet in the back of the neck. Why the bullet and the rope but not the gas? When I press the point, Richardi says to me, "It's like asking for proof that you've never beaten your wife."

Richardi cites several theories why the gas chamber was never put into operation. One holds that the camp commandant, Martin Gottfried Weiss, good SS man that he was, just couldn't bring himself to actually exterminate his charges en masse. "As camp commandant," observes Richardi, "if he had wanted this to happen, believe me, it would have happened." Another theory holds that by the time Baracke X was completed, the extermination facilities at Auschwitz were up and running and there was simply no need for the rather modest extermination plant in Dachau. "The Auschwitz gas chambers were much larger and more advanced than the one in Dachau," notes Richardi. "It was outdated by the time it was ready for operation." To Richardi's mind, the most compelling reason was that the SS barracks were literally "a stone's throw" from the gas chamber, and the Nazis did not want to risk poisoning their own people. Indeed, the facility was so close that Karl Huber, one of the Dachau *Häftlinge* involved in the gas chamber's construction, jokingly suggested to a fellow inmate that they divert the gas lines from the gas chamber into the SS barracks.

Although there seems to be no proof to suggest that mass exterminations took place, no one rules out the fact that the gas chamber found occasional use. Emma Wildenrotter told me that the gas chamber had been used two or three times for medical experiments with gas, but she differentiated between tests with poison gases for military purposes and the use of Zyklon B for mass extermination. Martin, of course, claims the gas chamber was used to kill all kinds of people and says he has the memories and nightmares to prove it.

Richardi disagrees with both Emma and Martin. While he concedes that the gas chamber may have seen occasional *"Versuchsvergasungen"*—test gassings—on clothing and vermin, as claimed by Franzicek Blaha, a Dachau survivor, he flatly rules out the idea that the gas chamber was used for any experiments with *Häftlinge*. "We had lots of medical experimentation here," Richardi says resolutely. "There were high-altitude experiments, and cold-water experiments, malaria experiments, and the operations on twins, pregnant women, and the handicapped, but I can assure you that there was absolutely no experimentation with poison gas for military purposes."

As I listen to Richardi and hear the frustration in his voice, I understand his need to do justice to historical reality. But I also understand the realities of public perception. Like the distinction drawn between Dachau as a "concentration camp" and Auschwitz as an "extermination camp," or the fact that a million people died in Auschwitz and "only" thirty-one or thirty-two thousand in Dachau, the debates surrounding the use of the Dachau gas chamber are essentially academic. Dachau, like Auschwitz, has assumed an iconic quality in our days, one that transcends rational understanding, one that has attached itself to a truth that overshadows any single fact or statistic.

17

ONE SUNNY AFTERNOON I ask Gertrud Schmidt-Podolsky if she thinks you have to be out of your mind—I use the German *verrückt*—in order to lead a normal life in Dachau. The blond firebrand of local politics, Schmidt-Podolsky has publicly championed the rights of Dachauers to live "normally despite their town's grim legacy."

"Do you have to be deranged to live a normal life in Dachau?" she repeats my question, pauses to let the words register, for herself and for me. I expect her to lay into me with the kind of self-righteous vitriol that she often hurls at members of the Town Council. But she does not. She brushes back her thick blond hair, and brandishing her razor-edged intellect like a threat, asks me, "Do you know what the word *deranged* means? Do you know what it is to be deranged?" Without waiting for an answer, Schmidt-Podolsky picks up an ashtray and plunks it down demonstratively on the table between us. "Everything has its range, its particular space," she says. "To be 'deranged' means to be out of place, to be displaced in relation to other objects. Like this." She slides the ashtray to the right of her coffee mug. "This ashtray was there, and now it's here. It has been 'deranged' in the literal sense of the word." She looks me straight in the eye to make certain her point has registered. "It is no longer where it was; however, in relation to itself, nothing has changed. It is still an ashtray. It is perfectly normal."

We are seated in her office on the third floor of the Dachau County Administrative building, a modern complex in a wooded neighborhood at the edge of town. On her wall is a poster from the 1995 Beijing Women's Conference. There are a few framed sketches by the Dachau artist Gigi, and along the windowsill several soapstone sculptures by her twenty-two-year-old daughter. They are hand-size abstract forms reminiscent of Henry Moore. On the door to her office is a sign that reads *"Frauenbeauftragte"*—Women's Affairs. As head of women's issues for the Town Council, Schmidt-Podolsky is responsible for making Dachau a better and safer place for women, for providing counseling for young girls, shelter for women who have been abused or sexually molested. "Dachau is a town just like any other town," Schmidt-Podolsky says. "And we have problems just like any other place in the world. It is my job to make Dachau a better and safer place for women to live and work."

Making Dachau a "better place" is something Schmidt-Podolsky has been doing since the age of seventeen, when her mother, then forty-three, gave birth to a "chromosome-damaged child." "I ran from office to office and discovered no one was willing to help my family, let alone help my sister," Schmidt-Podolsky recalls. "There were no special schools, no facilities for providing help or counseling. A handicapped child was something to be ashamed of, something to be hidden away. I swore that when I grew up I would do something to change all this."

Since 1976, when Schmidt-Podolsky was elected to the Town Council—at that time the only woman among the forty community leaders who gathered each month in the town hall to discuss taxes, sewage systems, and the price of beer at the annual Volksfest—Schmidt-Podolsky has emerged as a leading figure in the local conservative party. "I don't buy into the idea that we have to feel guilty living here," she says. "The majority of people alive in Dachau today were born after the war and have nothing to do with what happened in the camp." Her own family, she notes, comes from a German-speaking part of Poland that was not even part of Germany before the war. Neither of her grandfathers participated in the First World War, and her father had a disability that prevented him from fighting in the Second World War. "My father was not a 'bad German' or a 'good German,'" she says. "He was a sick German."

She defends those who want nothing more than to live "normal" lives in Dachau, and assails those Dachauers who attempt to make amends with the past and thereby "exploit" the memory of the dead and crippled. She speaks of local artists who "confront" the Holocaust in their paintings and sculptures, and then peddle it around the globe as "Dachau art." She rails in particular against the new mayor, Kurt Piller, whose recent trip to Israel she views as little more than a publicity stunt. "He keeps talking about the legacy of the Holocaust as providing a 'great opportunity' for the town of Dachau, but what does he mean by this?" she asks, her voice brimming with indignation. "He talks of the potential offered by the eight hundred thousand visitors who come to the camp each year. You ask if it is moral to live in Dachau and ignore the Holocaust, for a thirty-year-old mother to raise her two children in a safe and nurturing community? I ask *you:* Is it moral to promote the Holocaust in Dachau just so you can fill your shops and restaurants with tourists? I don't think so. In the end, you desecrate not only the memory of the thirty-three thousand people who died here but, in a sense, the memory of the other six million victims of the Holocaust."

That said, Schmidt-Podolsky concedes that living a normal life in Dachau is not the same as living normally elsewhere in Germany. Is it normal, she asks, that you cannot build a McDonald's in Dachau without causing an international incident? That the mayor cannot take a trip to Israel without it making headlines in the media? "If I intend to make an outrageous remark tomorrow afternoon about Israel or the Holocaust," Schmidt-Podolsky says, "I had better get my hair done in the morning, because the next day I will be all over the media." She pauses and moves the ashtray across the Formica tabletop. "Maybe this does not seem normal to you, but it is everyday life for us. Here in Dachau we know that things are different from what they are in Freising or Oberschleißheim or Munich. Dachau, you see, has its own particular normality. I call it *Dachauer Normalität.*"

Indeed it may seem incredible—or is the word "perverse" or "insane" or just plain "crazy"?—to the rest of the world for people to spend their lives in the shadow of the Holocaust, but it is indeed possible, and it is possible to live there quite nicely if you focus on your family, your work, and your community, and don't look too far beyond the corner of the Augsburger Strasse and the Kennedy Allee, where the city of Dachau ends and the rest of the world begins. The normal Dachauer does not wake up every morning wondering what it was like to rise at five in the morning in a wooden bunk in the camp in the dead of winter, or go to bed at night wondering if you will survive till dawn. They think about getting to work on time, about the price of that new dress at the Hörhammer department store, about their children's birthday parties, about their upcoming vacation to Spain or Italy, or about taking the car into the garage for servicing before winter sets in. On hot summer days, teenage girls slip into their bikinis and head for Karlsfelder Lake; on weekends, local bands take the stage at the Güterhalle, a converted warehouse beside the train station, bringing Dachau kids to their feet with high-decibel renderings of Elvis Presley hits that rattle the walls and waft across the heartless rails where boxcars once arrived packed with human cargo. Dachau kids, like most kids we know, just want to have fun. In fact, most Dachauers, Schmidt-Podolsky says, don't even give a passing thought to the camp and its dark legacy. They don't want to feel guilty or responsible or obligated to donate money for a tree on some forsaken hillside somewhere in the Middle East because of something that happened in Dachau over there across the railway tracks a half-century ago. "Der normale Dachauer will seine normale Dachauer Normalität einfach normal leben," Schmidt-Podolsky tells me in no uncertain terms—the normal Dachauer wants nothing more than to live his or her normal Dachau normality as normally as he or she can. No more and no less.

18

BARBARA DISTEL APOLOGIZES that her colleagues couldn't help me, and she is sorry that she cannot help me either, but the fact is that they have never been able to find Martin Zaidenstadt in the registry of names compiled from the Nazi registration cards after the war, and they are not about to begin looking now. A highly competent woman, Distel allocates her limited time and resources where they are most needed at a given moment. On this particular afternoon, a former Dachau *Häftling*, originally from the Ukraine but now living in Munich, is sitting in the reception area. Outside Distel's window, the camp grounds are teeming with busloads of visitors, as many as ten thousand a day on weekends, more than a hundred thousand a month in the summer. Her desk is covered with proofs for the pending issue of *Dachauer Hefte*, a monograph series she copublishes with Wolfgang Benz, an eminent Berlin-based scholar. Despite the stresses of overseeing a post-Holocaust tourist attraction, Barbara Distel looks great. On the day I visit, she is wearing a steel-blue silk blouse with complementing silk scarf, and a pair of mottled-blue eyeglass frames that contrast nicely with her short silver hair. Beneath these fashionable trappings is a tough and canny administrator. Having worked at the memorial site for more than a quarter-century, Distel has become adept at dealing with the neighboring town, with the state government of Bavaria, and, in particular, with the emotion-charged issues related to the Holocaust survivor community. On the day I visit she is in the middle of her ongoing struggle for adequate funding.

"The memorial site at Buchenwald has a staff of fifty-two and has half the number of visitors," Distel tells me. "I was recently at the Holocaust Museum in Washington. They have more than two hundred people working there." By comparison, Distel has but seven staffers to manage the mounting tide of mourners, sightseers, and returning survivors, including Martin Zaidenstadt.

Distel tells me that she had seen Martin now and again at commemoration events over the past twenty years, but three or four years ago he began to appear regularly outside the crematorium. He seemed a sweet, gentle man with a buoyant wit and an endearing smile who quickly won the affection of Distel's small staff. The groundskeeper, who has an office in a back room of the crematorium—the door to the right of the men's room—lets Martin rest on his sofa when he grows tired; the gray-haired saleslady at the museum's book counter frequently drives Martin home after working hours. The barrier rises for any vehicle bringing Martin to the gas chamber. Like the watchtowers, the barbed wire, the reconstructed barracks, crematorium, and gas chamber, Martin has become, in Distel's words, "part of the inventory."

Distel is not troubled by the dearth of documentation for this alleged survivor, or the absence of a number on his wrist—"Dachau inmates were not tattooed," she tells me—or the fact that other Dachau residents, like Hans Günter Richardi, who has interviewed dozens of survivors living in and around the Munich area, have never seen or heard of Martin Zaidenstadt. Or the fact that Martin's name does not appear in the camp registry. Not only is the list incomplete—as her deputy has already informed me—but Distel also believes that Martin may have been registered under a different name. When I volunteer to walk to the crematorium and ask him his real name, Distel says, "You need not do it for my sake." She is content knowing Martin for what he is—the survivor outside the gas-chamber door.

It is a ten-minute walk from Distel's office—located in the former SS administration building—across the *Appellplatz*, past the two reconstructed barracks, and down the "promenade" with its double rows of barrack foundations. In the distance, the concrete wall and watchtowers define the horizon. I tick off the rows of barracks like yard lines on a football field in a brisk, gravel-crunching march from Distel to Zaidenstadt.

When I arrive, Martin is standing near the wooden bridge that leads from the camp into the crematorium compound. It is a cold, wet autumn day with a slight bite to the air. Martin is wearing brand-new glasses, a fresh blue-gray tweed cap, and a worn tan trench coat that is buttoned tightly against the afternoon chill; the scuffed leather buttons twice sewn, once with tan thread, once with dark brown, dangle from the tattered buttonholes.

The scene is like a theatrical set piece. Martin stands, speaking in Hebrew—occasionally breaking into a wide grin when he chants or sings—to two couples from Israel, while a young man with three thick gold earrings and green hair looks on. Two Americans, a husband and wife, struggle irritably with their camcorder, casting furtive glances as Martin as if he is an apparition that will vanish before they can get the film rolling, and all the while a strikingly elegant Japanese woman, her flawlessly combed hair hanging straight down the back of her red wool coat, stands at a distance, the automatic flash on her digital camera blinking like the intermittent strobe of a lighthouse beacon. I join the queue behind a German couple with two preteen sons in time to hear the father whisper to his children, "Er ist ein echter Häftling." Martin, the real thing. After dispatching the two Israeli couples into the adjoining woods to see the execution sites, with their blood ditches and the stars of David carved in stone that mark the interred ashes of Jewish victims, Martin turns his attention to the young man with the earrings, who after a few minutes walks away, mournfully shaking his green head. Finally he makes his way to the German family. The father urges his sons forward and tells them to shake hands with the man. The conversation begins in German but quickly switches to Spanish when the father mentions that he has spent the last five years in Spain. After a few minutes the man murmurs to me, "His Spanish is better than his German." Emma Wildenrotter suddenly appears at the bridge, leading a troop of thirty German soldiers in gray uniforms with the crossed-swords emblem on their shoulders. She waves cheerily to Martin, calls out "Grüß Gott," and rushes the soldiers past him at double-step, then around a corner and into Crematorium I. Martin smiles at her and remarks, "She always waves to me." A few minutes later the two Israeli couples emerge from the woods, all four with stricken looks on their faces. One woman holds a tissue to her eyes.

As the German father speaks with Martin, he repeatedly glances as his two sons, who remain singularly unaffected by the historical import of this moment. They shuffle their feet in the gravel and bury their fists deep in their pockets. However, when the German man asks Martin if he was photographed during the liberation and Martin reaches into his coat pocket, their interest grows. I expect Martin to display his battered Rainbow Division card as evidence of his presence on liberation day, but instead he produces a packet of black-and-white photographs wrapped in a clear plastic bag.

Though I have witnessed Martin's diverse "routines" countless times, this one is new to me. Carefully he opens the bag, withdraws the stack of photographs, and shows them to the boys. Their interest is piqued for a brief moment, until they see it is only a photograph of the gate with an American soldier on either side and a cluster of inmates beyond. Martin points to a face in the crowd and says, "Das bin ich." The face is so small that it is indistinguishable from the hundred other blurred images. "Das bin ich," Martin repeats and smiles at the boys. The boys nod respectfully. The next photograph shows a heap of corpses, mouths agape, skin stretched over bones like dead cattle in a desert, and the one after that shows a group of *Häftlinge* in striped uniforms standing at the crematory oven, and then another of a single corpse, stripped naked, being dragged by an inmate with huge metal tongs that grip the skull. The head is dramatically twisted. As the two boys stare at the photographs in wide-eyed fascination, the mother and father glance at each other in mutual panic. The man interrupts Martin, thanks him for his time, and wishes him well. "Moment," Martin says as the man pulls away, the woman shepherding their children. He reaches into his pocket again, and this time produces a handful of hard candies wrapped in clear plastic. He hands three to each boy, and wishes them a nice day.

Two hours after setting off for the crematorium, I return to Barbara Distel with a jumble of names and information. Martin was born in 1911 in the village of Jedwabne, a small Jewish community set amid the cornfields of northeastern Poland. The son of a Jewish grain merchant, Martin grew up as Mordechai Zaidenstadt. During Poland's futile attempt to idle the German invasion of September 1939, he served in the 33rd Łomza Regiment. Following the Polish surrender, he was placed in a prisoner-of-war camp near Nowogrod. During a review of the prisoners, a German officer demanded that all Jews step forward. When the officer barked, "Juden austreten!" a Polish comrade seized Martin's arm and told him to remain silent; Martin was registered as the Polish soldier Mjetek Zaideta. Over the next three years, he was transferred to a series of work camps, near Berlin,

Cologne, and Paderborn, arriving in Dachau sometime in the autumn of 1943. Martin could not remember the exact day or month but recalled that the march from the train station to the camp was wet, cold, and muddy. When I asked him for the names of fellow inmates, he mentioned Borawski, Slaveko, and Czermanski. Except for Czermanski, Martin did not know their first names. They always called each other by the last name. Czermanski, however, was Jerzy, Jerzy Czermanski.

The search for Martin's alternate names in the camp registry is in vain, as is the search for Czermanski. We do, however, find a Borawski and a Slaveko.

Borawski	*13.6.24 Wierzbowo*	*100943*	*6.9.44 v. Natzw.*
Anton	*Wierzbowo*		*Sch.P. 16.9.44 n. Natzw.*

According to the camp registry, Anton Borawski had spent less than ten days in Dachau before being transferred to the Natzweiler concentration camp, leaving Distel to speculate that Martin had mistakenly recalled the name of Tadeusz Borowski, author of the classic Holocaust memoir *This Way to the Gas, Ladies and Gentlemen.*

There are two names listed under Slaveko: Eugenio, from Fontana, Italy, who died five days after the camp was liberated; and Antonio, from Trieste, beside whose name is the simple entry *"befr. Dachau"*—liberated from Dachau.

Standing over the tens of thousands of names in the camp registries that lie spread across the linoleum table beneath the cold glare of the fluorescent lights, I abandon myself to Distel's instinct that Martin is indeed a survivor. With Martin, do the facts really matter any longer? At eighty-seven years of age, he has defined himself as the man who is destined to spend the rest of his life outside the gas chamber door at Dachau. Does it really matter who he was or what he had done before this? Martin has moved beyond the facts of history and into the sheer undercurrent of a more profound emotional force. In his addled state, who is Martin, anyway? The man he thought he was or the man whose identity I wanted to find? Distel and I stand silently over the registry books for a moment. "Martin says he is a survivor," Distel eventually says. "If he thinks he is, and I don't have the records to prove that he is not, I must accept that he is." She pauses, then adds: "And anyway, at his age does it really matter?"

19

AN OVERCAST SUNDAY MORNING, and several hundred people crowd the area in front of Baracke X. Martin Zaidenstadt, dressed in a suit, stands on an elevated platform together with Max Mannheimer and Nikolaus Lehner—Dachau's three resident Holocaust survivors. A brass band pumps solemn music into the penetrating mist. It is the first Sunday in May, just days after the official liberation of the camp, and visitors have come from around Europe to mark, yet again, the anniversary of the camp's liberation by the 42nd Division on April 29, 1945. Several elderly men wear baseball caps with the Rainbow Division insignia, a red, green, and yellow stripe. Martin sits on the stand looking serious, solid, solemn, while Kurt Piller—the one with a light, youthful complexion that always looks freshly scrubbed— talks about responsibility, guilt, and memory.

When he has finished, the band strikes up the "Moorsoldaten"—"We are the Soldiers of the Moorlands"—the elegiac anthem the Dachau *Häftlinge* used to sing as they marched each day into the fields around Dachau. As the band plays, the crowd slowly disperses and the somber troop marches from the crematorium area to the *Appellplatz*, where an even larger crowd is assembled before a small forest of four-foot-high mourning wreaths. Following another round of speeches, this time about atrocity and courage and human fortitude, the crowd mingle like parishioners after the Sunday service. Groups of people cluster around the elderly Holocaust survivors. One spry survivor from Poland, dressed in a striped camp uniform with a matching striped cap pulled over his bald head, holds court before a large crowd, mostly Americans. He chats energetically with his audience, pausing occasionally to pose for a photograph with a man in a Dodgers cap, a woman in a Nike windbreaker, an entire family from Arkansas. There is a hearing aid imbedded in each of his rather large, protruding ears. "Segelohren," I hear one German teenager murmur—ears like sails.

There was a time in the early 1980s when some Dachauers believed that the day would come when the last Holocaust survivor would die, putting an end to "this entire pathetic parade" of former *Häftlinge* who return to Dachau each spring, drawing in their wake an army of Holocaust pilgrims and awakening dark, uncomfortable memories that most Dachauers are too senile to properly recall or are too young to have ever known. It was assumed there would be, in the words of one beer-swilling Dachauer, a "biological solution" to Dachau's "historic burden." Instead, it seems as if the fewer people there are who can actually remember, the more people there are who cannot forget.

One morning, a few days after the annual commemoration event at the former camp, I sit with Kurt Göttler over a cup of coffee in the editorial offices of the *Dachauer Nachrichten*. Since starting at the newspaper as a nineteen-year-old cub reporter, Göttler has emerged as the voice of indignant Dachau. He publicly laments the affronts Dachauers suffer in their daily lives, and he chastises those residents who insist on hanging out the town's dirty—or bloody—laundry.

When Bruno Schachtner, in an open letter to the *Dachauer Neueste*, recounted his father's career as an SS officer in Dachau, igniting a debate about local complicity with the Nazis, Göttler castigated Schachtner for opening old wounds for town and family. "Does Bruno Schachtner actually know what he has done with his letter not only to Dachau but also to his own mother?" Göttler asked in a commentary, expressing pity for the widow of the former SS officer who had to witness her very own son raise issues that, according to Göttler, had been addressed and resolved a half-century earlier. "It is well known that there are people outside Dachau who are always ready to stir up these matters," Göttler concluded. "But the fact that Schachtner, a Dachauer, has fanned these flames is beyond comprehension." It is fitting that this particular debate was framed by a letter in the *Dachauer Neueste*, and a response in the *Dachauer Nachrichten*.

On the day we meet, Göttler is venting his frustrations over the town of Weimar, the home of Goethe and Schiller and birthplace of Germany's first and abortive attempt at democracy, which was also home to Germany's second most notorious concentration camp, Buchenwald. "I took a tour of the city," Göttler tells me, "and during the entire time the guide did not make a single reference to the concentration camp. There was not a single sign indicating the presence of a concentration camp, and yet Buchenwald is just as close to Weimar as the concentration camp here is to Dachau. Can you imagine what people would say if we gave a tour of Dachau and failed to mention the camp?"

Göttler then launches into a tirade against a host of other German cities that have cast off their pre-1945 identity and redefined themselves for the postwar world: Munich, the former "capital" of the Nazi movement, which is now renowned for its Hofbräuhaus and Oktoberfest; Nürnberg, the host to the annual Nazi rallies and backdrop for Leni Riefenstahl's film *Triumph of the Will*, which now markets its gingerbread cookies and Christmas Market; and Berlin, the twelve-year capital of the thousand-year Reich, which has, since the fall of the Berlin Wall, become a symbol of unity and freedom. Why, Göttler wonders, can Leonard Bernstein stand on the very site of Hitler's Reich Chancellery and conduct Beethoven's Ninth Symphony, but the Beaux Arts Trio of New York will refuse to perform in the Dachau Schloss because of the horrors committed there?

According to Göttler, Dachau's new mayor, Kurt Piller, is not helping matters any by planting trees in Israel and talking about Dachau's "great opportunity." While the rest of Germany is rushing to outstrip its Nazi past, Piller is pointing the town full speed into the past. He has published a three-hundred-page guide to Dachau written by Hans Günter Richardi that details virtually every aspect of town life under the Nazis; he is promoting a Youth Guest House that regularly features special events related not just to the Holocaust but to other atrocities, ranging from the extermination of the American Indians to the slaughter in Bosnia and Rwanda. "I am not saying that we should ignore what happened here," Göttler tells me, "but I also don't think we should have to bear the entire burden for what happened in Germany under the Nazis." This, according to Göttler, is not only unfair, it is also a dangerous development.

"To my mind this is a very bad strategy that can have very dangerous long-term consequences," Göttler observes. "The more Dachau becomes singularly associated with the Holocaust, the more you see people using the concentration camp as a platform for their particular political cause. We have had a conference here on the persecution of homosexuals around the world, and another one on the persecution of Gypsies and one on the extermination of the American Indians." Göttler glares at me, his face ablaze, and asks. "What, I ask you, does Dachau have to do with the killing of American Indians? What does that have to do with Dachau? We have enough problems of our own to solve without taking on the problems of the entire world."

Göttler fears that in the course of time, it will only get worse. As times passes, people will forget about the other concentration camps—names like Mauthausen and Neuengamme and Sachsenhausen—and in the end there will remain only two names associated with the Holocaust—Dachau and Auschwitz—the first and the largest. The more attention becomes focused on Dachau, the greater the temptation will be for people seeking to make a political statement to exploit Dachau. This is already the case. When the Bonn government prepared to expel several hundred Gypsies from Germany, the protesters descended on Dachau and occupied the barracks in the concentration camp. With the international media swarming over the camp, the police did not even consider removing the protesters from the barracks.

"If someone hangs himself in the Dachau moors," Göttler concludes, "it will most likely make it into our newspapers here in town. If someone hangs himself in the Dachau old town, it will probably make it into the Munich newspapers. But if someone hangs himself in front of the concentration camp memorial site, the next day it will be on the front page of the *New York Times*."

20

IF YOUR CHILD HAS RESPIRATORY PROBLEMS, either a temporary rattling in the chest or a chronic case of asthma, open the Dachau telephone directory to the section titled "Ärzte" and call Hans Joachim Sewering, Professor Dr. Dr. med. Internist, Lungen- und Bronchialheilkunde. As Dachau's leading respiratory specialist, Sewering has, since establishing his practice here after the war, helped generations of Dachau residents breathe easier. "He is without a doubt one of Dachau's most prominent citizens, who is also renowned in Bavaria and around the country," a local newspaper observed three years ago, on the occasion of Sewering's eightieth birthday. In the course of his remarkably productive career, Sewering garnered titles, positions, and distinctions the way Soviet generals once collected war medals. He has served as a member of the Bavarian Senate, as president of the German Medical Association, and, between 1958 and 1993, in senior posts in the World Medical Association. He is also a recipient of the Bavarian Service Medal, the Bavarian State Medal for Social Services, the Bavarian Constitutional Medal in silver and gold, the Bundesverdienstkreuz with star and shoulder banner—Germany's highest civilian distinction—as well as the Great Service Award of the Republic of Italy. However, in July 1995, the United States bestowed on Sewering his most notable distinction when the U.S. Justice Department's Office of Special Investigations—charged with hunting down Nazi war criminals—placed him on their Watch List, where the Dachau physician currently finds himself in the company of suspected terrorists, drug dealers, and former Nazis, including Austria's Kurt Waldheim.

"To put someone on the Watch List is a good-faith belief that the person may have been involved in persecution under Nazi regimes which would make him ineligible to come to the United States," observes Allan Ryan, the former OSI director who first logged suspected Nazi war criminals onto the Watch List roster. "But it is not in itself a determination of guilt." In the case of Sewering, that process has been assumed by Michael Franzblau. "It is my belief that Dr. Sewering participated voluntarily in a program called T-4 in which doctors killed their patients with disabilities in order to 'cleanse the Fatherland,'" says Franzblau, a California physician who lost twenty-five family members to a Wehrmacht killing unit in July 1942. "Until physicians like Dr. Sewering acknowledge their guilt, show remorse for their actions, and apologize to the surviving families of the defenseless children who were killed by physicians, there will be an ethical cloud over all physicians in Germany." For the last six years, Franzblau has led a relentless campaign to bring Sewering to justice. He has rallied scores of U.S. physicians to his cause, traveled repeatedly to Germany to lobby government officials, and hired a Munich lawyer who has drafted a forty-four-page legal brief outlining Sewering's alleged criminal activity. All in vain. "The German officials could not be more polite and friendly," Franzblau says. "They spend time driving me around in their BMWs, but end up telling me there is nothing they can do." In July 1995, Franzblau vented his mounting frustration in a $62,500 full-page advertisement in the *New York Times.*

WHY IS THE GERMAN STATE OF BAVARIA HARBORING AN ACCUSED WAR CRIMINAL?

The German State of Bavaria is harboring and protecting a war criminal.

The German State of Bavaria has protected Dr. Hans Joachim Sewering for 50 years.

Dr. Hans Joachim Sewering is accused of participating in the transfer of 900 German Catholic children from Schoenbrunn Sanatorium to a "Healing Center" at Eglfing-Haar, where they died.

Four nuns made this allegation in January 1993.

They were eyewitnesses to these crimes and broke their vow of silence 50 years after the fact at the suggestion of the Bishop of Munich.

Dr. Sewering, age 78, still practices medicine in Dachau.

Dr. Sewering must be brought to the bar of justice now.

The relatives of the murdered children ask for justice.

*The German people will be cleansed of this stain on their honor by
the successful prosecution and conviction of Dr. Hans Joachim
Sewering for murder and crimes against humanity.*

The advertisement, signed by 125 American physicians, was followed by similar paid announcements
throughout the United States and in Germany. While
the campaign exposed Sewering to the klieg-light glare
of media attention, including a segment on the CBS
news magazine *60 Minutes*, it has had no tangible juridi-
cal consequences in Bavaria.

Today, Sewering continues to practice medicine publicly and profitably in a modern three-story clinic in a
quiet wooded Dachau neighborhood, a pleasant five-
minute walk from the railway station. According to the
brass plaque on his office door, Doctor Sewering sees
patients on Mondays, Wednesdays, and Fridays, generally in the afternoon, or by appointment. When I called
his office one Wednesday to arrange an interview, the
receptionist told me Sewering was not in and suggested
I call back at four o'clock that same afternoon. In antici-
pation of the call, I sent Sewering a fax explaining that I
was writing a book on Dachau, had spoken with many
prominent citizens in town, and hoped to meet with
him, ideally the following day. When I called back at
four o'clock, the receptionist informed me that Sewering would not be available the next day. I then asked if

another day might be better, and listened as the receptionist set down the phone to consult with Sewering. He informed her that there was no convenient time, and she in turn got back to me with the message that the good doctor was not giving interviews.

One cannot blame Sewering for his vow of silence. The Dachau doctor is still stinging from the last in-depth interview he gave, in January 1993 to the *Dachauer Neueste*'s Tom Soyer. At the time, Sewering, then president-elect of the World Medical Association, found himself battling the ghosts of his Nazi past. When charges of Sewering's Nazi collaboration first emerged, the physician dismissed them, saying he had joined the Reiter SS—a relatively benign Nazi riding club—as "the most comfortable way" to pass the war years. In response, the German weekly *Der Spiegel* reminded Sewering that he had, in fact, also been in the regular SS, that his membership number was 143,000, that he served that criminal organization as an *SS-Mann* in the 2. Sturm of the I. Sturmbann of the 31st SS-Standarte, that he was also registered with the Nazi Party, that his membership number was 1858805, and further, that he had held membership in yet another Nazi organization, the Altherrenbund, and that while in Munich he occupied an apartment in the SA-Hochschulamt, a sister organization of the SS. Most damning of all, Sewering was found to have been the chief physician at a medical facility that between 1940 and 1944 dispatched more than nine hundred handicapped children to a neighboring euthanasia clinic.

Appalled at the prospect of a former SS doctor overseeing a medical organization founded with the express purpose of protecting patients from medical abuses, the American Medical Association, spurred by Michael Franzblau, demanded Sewering's resignation as president-elect of the World Medical Association. Rallying behind their besieged colleague, Karsten Vilmar, president of the German Medical Association, dismissed the allegations as a "slander campaign." Sewering himself spoke of a "world Jewish conspiracy." In January 1993, as the ghosts from Sewering's Nazi past spooked the international medical community, Tom Soyer, sitting at his desk at the *Dachauer Neueste*, called Sewering across town and asked if he would be willing to give an in-depth interview on his Nazi past. To Soyer's astonishment, Sewering agreed.

"Professor Sewering, you have been accused by your colleagues of having been implicated in a case of so-called euthanasia," Soyer said to the seventy-eight-year-old physician the next day. "It has to do with the case of Babette F., who on November 1, 1943, was transferred from the tuberculosis clinic at Schönbrunn, where you were working, to Eglfing-Haar, where she died fifteen days later. The 'medical record' for her transfer bears your signature."

With a fatherly air, the bulky Sewering, seated at his desk and wearing his white medical coat, explained to Soyer that the clinic in Schönbrunn had been for tuberculosis patients as well as for physically and mentally handicapped girls who were attended by Catholic nuns, while the clinic in Eglfing had been a psychological clinic to which troublesome patients were sometimes transferred. But as Sewering well knew, and as Soyer reminded him, the Eglfing-Haar clinic had been re-tooled as a euthanasia facility under the auspices of Hermann Pfannmüller, a fanatic Nazi doctor who even after 1941, when the Nazis officially suspended their euthanasia program—owing to protests by clerics and the public—continued to exterminate his charges in a special *"Hungerhaus"* in which patients were gradually starved to death over a two-to-three-week period. The method required neither poisons nor injections, and was subtle enough to avoid attention by the "certain gentle-men in Switzerland," Pfannmüller's term for Red Cross inspectors. "Our method is much simpler and more nat-ural," Pfannmüller boasted to a visitor who toured his facility. Standing beside a bed in the children's ward, Pfannmüller had an emaciated child dangled before his guests "as if it were a dead rabbit," observing casually, "With this one, for example, it will take another two to three days." The Pfannmüller diet was simple and deadly effective.

According to medical records discovered in the Eglfing-Haar archives, Babette Fröwis, a fourteen-year-old mentally handicapped girl, was transferred from Schönbrunn to Eglfing-Haar in the autumn of 1943. Two accompanying full-length nude photographs, one from the front and one from the side, show a lanky, flat-chested teenager with thick, dark hair cut in a pageboy style. She holds her right arm rigidly at her side; her left hand is held unconsciously over her genitals. She smiles

uncertainly at the camera, an expression of sweet bewilderment on her face. A "transfer document," dated
November 1, 1943, reads:

> *Babette Fröwis, born July 7, 1929, has been in the Schön-*
> *brunn clinic since September 13, 1934. She suffers from*
> *epilepsy and erratic idiocy. Since Fröwis has become*
> *excitable and is no longer fit for Schönbrunn, she is to be*
> *transferred to the appropriate department at the Eglfing-*
> *Haar Sanatorium.*

Two weeks after her arrival in Eglfing-Haar, Babette
was dead. The final entry in her medical record, dated
November 16, 1943, reads: "For the last five days, inad-
equate consumption of nutrition, chokes frequently
while eating. In recent days, tracheobronchial syndrome.
Today, exitus." Babette, in fact, did not succumb to star-
vation; she had to be killed. Despite the corrosive effects
of the malnutrition that eventually drew her into a
comatose state, Babette refused to die, and so, on the
morning of November 16, her caretakers administered
an injection of Luminal, a powerful sedative that caused
cardiac arrest. Babette died within minutes.

When Soyer noted that the Fröwis transfer document, which served in fact as a death sentence, bore
Sewering's signature, the Dachau doctor responded
blithely, "Naturally, because a physician has to sign the
transfer document. The physician has to do that, and I
was the assistant doctor, and so I had to sign the document for the nuns." When Soyer insisted that his signature represented a "medical decision" on his part,

Sewering corrected him: "No, things were back then the way they are today: if a nurse in a sanatorium cannot deal with a patient, and they can no longer properly care for them, then there isn't anything else left to do but transfer them."

"But what sense does it make to transfer a patient from a long-term care facility," Soyer demanded, "because someone believes the person cannot be cured?"

"You have to distinguish," Sewering replied with a patronizing air. "Schönbrunn is a sanatorium. Haar is a psychological clinic, and has completely different possibilities for dealing with patients who could harm themselves or others. The nuns acted in good conscience, and if the nuns made a particular request, then you could trust them. The working relationship was that good—it still is. Even today I still serve as the consulting physician there." Sewering paused, looked at Soyer, and said, his voice filling with self-righteous indignation, "If you mean to suggest that the nuns knowingly sacrificed a patient, then I have to speak in their defense. No one knew what was happening."

Five years later, Soyer still expresses quiet astonishment at Sewering's absence of personal responsibility or even the faintest glimmer of remorse for the deaths of his charges. Though Soyer pressed the former SS doctor, Sewering continued to insist that both the nuns who proposed the transfers and the physicians who signed the orders had no idea what lay in wait for their charges in Eglfing-Haar. The nuns who worked under Sewering, it turned out, remembered things quite differently.

Two days after the *Dachauer Neueste* ran the Sewering interview, Soyer received a punishing letter from Sister Benigna Sirl, head of the Schönbrunn Sanatorium, denouncing Sewering's assertion that the nuns had acted in "good conscience." The nuns, she insisted, knew exactly what was happening in Eglfing-Haar. "The nuns knew all too well that these severely mentally and physically handicapped human beings were to be destroyed as so-called worthless life," she wrote, insisting that the sisters did everything in their power to prevent the transfer of their charges—altering medical records, sending severely handicapped children back home—but that despite their efforts, the SS doctors continued to transfer large numbers of handicapped girls to Eglfing-Haar, 203 on the occasion of Hitler's fiftieth birthday, and 179 more just two day before Christmas 1943. "In spite of the fact that this happened so long ago," Sirl wrote, "those nuns who are still living continue to suffer deeply from the terrifying scenes that played themselves out with these transfers."

The Sewering interview coupled with Sirl's damning response proved a toxic combination. Within days, Sewering had resigned from the World Medical Association, and the Jewish Defense League was demanding that the U.S. Justice Department launch an investigation into his Nazi past. By July, the Dachau lung specialist had been inducted into the notorious ranks of the department's Watch List. Sewering has fared better in Bavaria. Despite intensive investigations into Sewering's complicity in the Nazi euthanasia program, the Bavarian state prosecutor's office insists it cannot find enough evidence to bring the former SS doctor to trial. Although

Franzblau insists that Bavaria is protecting a euthanasia murderer, Soyer supports the prosecutor's decision.

"I had access to the records in Haar, and after going through the files, I arrived at the same opinion as the Bavarian justice system," notes Soyer. "Namely, that Sewering did not perform euthanasia murders. He was not someone who injected handicapped children with Luminal or let them starve to death in a hunger house. The evidence we have simply indicates that he signed a document that Babette Fröwis should be transferred from Schönbrunn to Haar." Like it or not, Soyer argues, this is not enough information on which to accuse someone of murder. "The question is, did he know what he was doing when he signed that document? Did he know that he was sealing the fate of Babette Fröwis, this fourteen-year-old handicapped girl, or did he simply think that he was transferring her to another clinic? Regardless of what anyone thinks or wants to think, we have no evidence and no witnesses that say 'Dr. Hans Joachim Sewering signed the transfer document because he felt obligated to do so by the Nazi ideology.' We simply lack this evidence, and in a society governed by the rule of law we must accept this fact."

Soyer pauses uncomfortably for a moment before continuing: "Please understand that I don't have an especially good feeling about all this. I would feel better if Sewering had somehow come clean, had condemned what happened, had said something like 'It was horrible, and we all knew that the Nazis viewed the mentally handicapped as worthless life'"—Soyer uses the term *unwertes Leben*—"'and wanted to eliminate them, and naturally you found yourself caught in the chain of decisions, but there was simply nothing you could do about it at the time.' If he had said something like that, if he had expressed regret, and had said explicitly, 'It is terrible that such a thing could have happened, and in retrospect I damn it with all my heart, and it hurts me beyond belief that I was also a cog in that horrible machinery.' If he had said something like this, then I would have the highest respect for him—then I would say, Okay, he has in a way restored his honor. But he was incapable of doing this, and tried to talk his way out of it, tried to suppress it." Soyer pauses again, and adds bitterly, "Er lebt mit einer Lebenslüge"—He lives his life as a lie.

21

FOR THE LAST SEVERAL WEEKS, my search for Martin Zaidenstadt has been fruitless. After failing to find Martin in the Dachau archives, I call the Suchstelle near Hannover, the Red Cross office responsible for tracking the six million known Holocaust survivors. They, however, cannot help me. They can release information only to survivors themselves and to immediate family members. I call Steven Spielberg's Shoah Memorial Project, which has an archive of more than fifty thousand interviews with Holocaust survivors, and am told that although Martin registered to give his testimony, he later changed his mind. The Fortunoff Memory Project at Yale University, which has been collecting interviews with Holocaust survivors since 1984, also has no record of Martin, but the project director Joanne Rudof comforts me.

When I explain to her that I am having difficulty confirming the identity of an alleged Holocaust survivor, that some people have suggested that he is an imposter, and that his testimony is indeed riddled with inconsistencies, Rudof tells me that my experience with Martin is hardly unusual. As survivors age, their memories blur, and they often incorporate information they have heard or read from others into their own experience. Like Distel, Rudof relies on her instincts to determine the credibility of individual survivors. When a story strains credibility, Rudof cuts it from the archive. For example, one elderly woman who claimed to be an Auschwitz survivor recalled how Adolf Eichmann had severely gashed himself while visiting Auschwitz and she was called on to suture his wound. In another case, an American veteran claimed that he had been among the soldiers who helped liberate Auschwitz, which in fact was liberated by the Russians, and then went on to testify that he had also discovered Jews crucified on crosses in a cave, and had subsequently met the "man behind Hitler," a large, sinister figure over seven feet tall. Rudof also tells me of a Jewish man who, following his release from Sobibor, went to California and became a successful businessman, only to move back to the former death camp, where he now, like Martin, passes his days talking to visitors.

Rudof then mentions that after the war hundreds of survivors began assembling Yizkor books. As the Hebrew name Yizkor—memory—suggests, these books are intended to preserve the memory of the Jewish communities that vanished in the wake of the Holocaust. They are published by small presses, primarily in New York and Israel, in extremely low print runs and are filled with histories, anecdotes, photographs, maps, and genealogies, whatever scraps of fact and memory remain from these obliterated communities. There are hundreds of Yizkor books, mostly published in Hebrew and Yiddish, sometimes in Polish or Ukrainian, but only occasionally in English. Given that Jedwabne had fewer than 1,600 Jews, Rudof says it is unlikely that there was ever a Yizkor book put together for this particular town. The following morning I receive an e-mail message from Rudof that begins: "I struck gold." There is not only a Yizkor book on Jedwabne, it was published relatively recently, in 1980—and, best of all, it is available in English. She has located copies at several libraries in the United States, including the Holocaust Museum in Washington and the Hebrew University of Ohio. She also says the Bialik Institute in Israel stocks Yizkor books. Within a week, I have a copy of *Yedwabne: History of a Shtetl and Its People.*

The book on Jedwabne—in Yiddish, Yedwabne— confirms much of what Martin has told me about this peaceful, prosperous, and proud community a two-hour drive north of Warsaw, where the Poles tended the fields and the Jews plied the trades. Along the unpaved streets of this dusty village, Jewish cobblers, barrelmakers, carpenters, tailors, wheelwrights, saddlers, and ironsmiths earned their living in tidy family shops. "Yedwabne shoes, clothing and furniture were renowned," the Yizkor book proudly records. "A Yedwabne spinning wheel was valued for the perfection of its construction and the precision of its yarns." It was said of the Jedwabne Jews that they obeyed the laws and prayed daily to Jehova and never broke the Sabbath. The book mentions numerous local families, the harnessmaker Yakov Katz, the "stitcher" Eli Krawiecki, the blacksmith Shmuel Weinstein, and the businessmen Moshe Fishman and Choneh Goldberg. There is no mention of the grain trader Abraham Zaidenstadt.

There is, however, an entire chapter devoted to

Avigdor Bialystocky, "the last Rabbi of Yedwabne," that confirms everything Martin has told me about this wise and gentle cleric who maintained an abiding faith in the goodness of mankind. "Although he was a Chasid and went occasionally to the Rebbe of Slonim, he did not impose Chasidism on his Kehila," the book notes. "He was a very close friend of the Rabbi Yechiel Mordechai Gordon, dean of the Yeshiva of Łomza, and was admired by the Yeshiva students." Even more importantly, Bialystocky maintained close ties with the Catholic bishop of Łomza. In early summer of 1941, when a pogrom ravaged the Jewish community in the neighboring town of Wisno, Bialystocky traveled to Łomza to meet with the bishop. In exchange for a tithe, the bishop guaranteed the safety of Bialystocky's community.

Days later rumors circulated in Jedwabne that the Poles had petitioned the Germans to purge Jedwabne of its Jews. Bialystocky dismissed these concerns. The bishop, he said, had promised to protect them. A man of the cloth, regardless of his persuasion, could be trusted to keep his word. Even on the morning of July 10, 1941, the fifteenth day of Tammuz, when Piotr Karoliak, Jedwabne's notoriously anti-Semitic chief magistrate, ordered the Jews of Jedwabne to assemble in the town square, the rabbi kept his faith in his bishop. By eleven o'clock, with nearly fifteen hundred men, women, and children assembled in the blazing midsummer heat, Rabbi Bialystocky wandered among his parishioners, calming their fears, assuring them that the bishop of Łomza was a good and honest man, that he had given his word that the Jews of Jedwabne would be safe. But as the day wore on, and the heat intensified, and the throng of gentiles grew increasingly belligerent, the mood turned ominous, then violent.

"They selected forty people at a time and sent them to the cemetery, where they were forced to dig ditches in which they were buried alive," recalls one survivor. "They put a big stone on the head of Rabbi Avigdor Bialystocky and made him carry it through the marketplace. The goyim grabbed Yudke Nadolnic's daughter Gitele, cut off her head, and played with it as it if was a ball." Survivors report diverse acts of savagery against the assembled Jews throughout the afternoon. Toward nightfall, a man by the name of Weshilewski appeared on the square and loudly proclaimed a death sentence upon the rabbi and his Jews. "Because you are decent Jews," Weshilewski said, "we have chosen for you an easy way to die." The Poles then fell upon the Jews with knives and clubs, driving them down the Ulica Nowa to the edge of town, where they were forced into the Shelmanski barn. The building was then doused with canisters of benzine and set ablaze. "Some of us succeeded in running into the cornfields," recalls Moshe Kochev, who survived the pogrom. "Many were caught and killed on the spot. Those of us in the fields could hear the rabbi saying Vidui with the people, and then we saw smoke rise, and then came the smell of burning flesh." Michael Kuropatve, the wagondriver, who had once saved a Polish pilot from the Russians in the war of 1921, was told that his life would be spared. "I do not want to live a life given to me by murderers," he said and walked back into the barn followed by his wife and daughter.

"I learned about the burning from a man named Koselski," Martin says. "He had worked for my father and used to bring the grain with his wagon from Jedwabne to the train station in Łomza. He was a prisoner in Feldafing, near Dachau. He recognized me and told me that my entire family had been put into a barn and burned." In 1976, Martin returned to Jedwabne to look for traces of his former life. When he knocked on the door of his family home, a pleasant Polish man opened the door and invited him into the house to have a look, but Martin was so overcome with emotion that he declined the offer. When the local police caught him photographing the village square and interrogated him, he was so unnerved that he and his wife got into their car and drove through the night until they reached the German border.

22

THE TRUCK ROARS PAST, leaving me choking in a whirl-wind of diesel and dust as the rented Fiat Brava lurches down the road toward Jedwabne. An elderly Polish woman in a red kerchief rakes leaves beside a table-size satellite dish while chickens peck and scratch at the bare soil. Beside a collapsed brick house a white sign marks the city limits of Jedwabne. It is late Monday morning, and my father and I have been on the road for more than two hours, driving northeast from Warsaw to an obscure pocket of Poland tucked in the northern shoulder where Poland meets Russia, Lithuania, and Belarus, a rather rough neck of the Central European woods. Knowing the anti-Semitic tendencies among many Poles, and not wanting to depend on a local translator who might filter or dodge, I have enlisted the services of my father, a retired attorney and son of Polish immigrants who grew up speaking the language of the homeland. Previously a tense, cynical man who lived by the motto "I don't get ulcers, I give them," two recent strokes, along with daily doses of blood-thinners and heart-regulating drugs—Coumadin, Dilantin, and Lanoxin—have mellowed him into a charmingly distracted senior citizen in a forest-green cashmere coat and a matching fedora that he occasionally forgets to remove even after he has hung up his coat. Yet when he needs to focus, his mind can cut like a razor.

For the first hour out of Warsaw we drove along a well-kept three-lane road lined with newly constructed houses, billboards, commercial ventures, and endless fields with some of the richest farming soil in all Europe. While grim, stooped, God-fearing women, their thick figures wrapped in gray and brown dresses, glean the last harvest of potatoes from the cold earth, teenage hookers in short orange and green fluorescent miniskirts stand along the roadside in groups of two and three, chatting with one another, pausing to lift their skirts or hold out a slender leg for the occasional passing car or truck, then returning to their cheerful banter.

At an intersection in the town of Ostrow Mazowiecka, just beyond a shop that advertises handmade wooden coffins—*wytwor trumnów*—we turn on the road to Łomza. The landscape opens into vast expanses of carefully tilled fields, then a patchwork of forests and small villages with church steeples rising against the gray autumn sky, awaking in my father a flood of stories from our own ancestral roots in the Polish hinterland. Ryback derives from the Slavic word *ryba*—fish. For the next hour my father recounts stories of Polish resourcefulness in the face of tsars, kaisers, and Communists, all of which at one time or another have dispatched tax collectors to exact fiscal blood from the hardworking people. My father hates tax collectors regardless of race, creed, or ideology.

Jedwabne is little more than a tic-tac-toe grid of streets set with shops and modest two-story houses. A handsome white church with elegant twin spires dominates the town square, a grand presence in an otherwise somber setting. On one corner, a horse-drawn wooden wagon with rubber tires stands abandoned; on another, a rusting tractor has a Hudson Bay blanket—a gift perhaps from some relative in Canada—tossed over its engine. In front of the church Gypsies hawk assorted goods from the hood of a car: a set of screwdrivers, some drill bits, a camshaft, and packages of Marlboro cigarettes. Little kids dressed in ragged clothes kick balls in the streets. The ubiquitous elderly men and women watch this intruder with Warsaw license plates drive haltingly through the streets.

We head straight for the town hall, a one-story brick building on the edge of town. The only bit of color is a white Polish eagle against a red background. We enter the mayor's office and inform the secretary that we are looking for former Jedwabne residents who had served in the 33rd Łomza Regiment and ask to speak with the mayor. We are promptly told by the secretary—a thickset woman in a tight black acrylic sweater with dyed red hair and too much perfume—that the mayor is not in, that she does not know when he will be in, that she cannot really help us. This much I am able to decipher from the series of "No, no, no" that issues forth. My father smiles and begins to chat with her. I repeatedly hear the words *pierogi* and *kapusta*, the two favorite dishes from my father's childhood. Before I know it, the woman is chattering away, smiling, and a few minutes later, is on the telephone. When she hangs up, she informs us that we should go have lunch and come back in an hour and a half.

We lunch in the neighboring town of Wizna, where we find a "resztaurant" that appears to be little more than an unheated garage with a bar, two meagerly stocked shelves of snacks, and a dozen or so patrons, all men, bundled in soiled jackets with wool caps pulled over their ears. An electric space heater with half the elements missing is the only source of warmth. To cut the chill, the beer is served hot. My father walks straight to the bar, orders a round of drinks for everyone in the establishment, including the bartender, then sits down at a table with three brutish men who when they smile have no more than eight or nine teeth among them. When my father mentions we are looking for veterans of the 33rd Łomza Regiment, it unleashes a torrent of war stories that does not abate for the next hour. Though none of the men served in the 33rd Łomza, they had all fought as partisans, and they speak avidly about the brutality of the Russians, the viciousness of the Germans, and the betrayal of the Jews. The Russians, we are told, would come into town, look at the hands of every man they could find, and if he did not have calluses would execute him on the spot as an intellectual. Anyone who escaped this test was handed over to the Russians by the Jews.

As I smell the hatred of the Jews on their sour breath, listen to the animosity hissing through each gap-toothed word, and feel the winter chill gnawing at my legs and back, I sense how vulnerable the hundreds of

Jewish shtetls must have been in this remote corner of Central Europe. For centuries, they had entrusted their fates to the goodness of God and the benevolence of the Polish peasants, only to find their trust betrayed.

After an hour, we take our leave, cold, hungry, and tipsy, and return to Jedwabne, where the mayor is waiting, a cheerful man in his mid-forties who is taking distance-education classes by computer—"I am looking for a real job." He says that he knows of no Jedwabne citizens who served in the 33rd Łomza Regiment, and unfortunately the town has no archival materials. Most were destroyed when Jedwabne, caught between the Germans and the Russians during the First World War, was virtually leveled by artillery bombardments. The rest were either destroyed by the Germans at the beginning of the Second World War, or hauled off by the Russians at war's end. He does, however, get on the phone to Jerzy Ramatowski, the local German teacher who also serves as the town historian. Within five minutes Ramatowski is standing in the office with a sixty-page typescript history of Jedwabne.

While my father and the mayor argue about school education—the mayor maintains that if you overeducate the youth of Jedwabne they will leave town and never come back—Ramatowski reviews with me his history of Jedwabne, which he wrote in the late 1970s. He readily concedes that relations were not always good between the Poles and the Jews. "When the Russians came into Jedwabne, the Jews handed over lists of all the Polish intellectuals," he tells me. "The Russians rounded them up, took them to Russia, and executed them. Not a single one ever returned." When I ask if this act of betrayal justified the Poles cramming the town's entire Jewish population into a barn, dousing it with benzine, and burning them alive, he informs me that the Germans had murdered Jedwabne's Jews, not the Poles. When I inform him that the Jewish survivors had reported that it was the Poles, not the Germans, who had staged the pogrom, he looks at me and says matter-of-factly, "The Jews have their memories, and we have ours."

Ramatowski then offers to take me on a tour of the village. The site of the former synagogue is now little more than a cobblestone alley with buildings—apparently from the 1950s—pressed up on either side so there is just enough space to drive a car through it. On the town square, where the Jewish population was gathered on that blazing July afternoon while Rabbi Bialystocky was humiliated before his people and forced to carry a stone on his head, there is a pleasantly planted park with large trees. Ramatowski points vaguely to the shops and says that many of them were owned by Jews. He really does not know which. A new three-story house is being constructed on a plot of land just to the right of the church, where Martin said his family house used to stand.

We then march down the Ulica Drobna, past six houses, turn left down the Ulica Tukil, past a butcher's shop and a car repair service, where the town abruptly ends and the fields begin. A short way up the street, a heavily rutted dirt road veers to the right and strikes out across a barren stretch of brown fields, turned under for the winter and covered with a dusting of light snow. A quarter-mile down this road is a small black monument marking the place where, according to the text on the monument, twelve hundred Jedwabne Jews were murdered by the Hitlerites and their gendarmes. It is a small stone monument. Several spent memorial candles mark the site. Just beyond the monument stand the tumbled ruins of a stone barn. When I suggest that it is most likely the barn where the burning took place, Ramatowski corrects me. No, that barn belongs to the Szubaskis. The burning took place right on the spot where we are standing. It was a wooden barn, without any foundation. Unlike Pompeii, the scorching death that obliterated the Jews of Jedwabne has left no trace. There are no stone-cast children clinging in their agony to their mothers' skirts; there are no men with arms upstretched in smoke-choked appeals to a merciful God. On this desolate patch of Polish earth, there is only stiff grass and frozen ground. The piled corpses with their charred bones and baked and blistered skin have, like their screams and prayers, vanished in time or been buried deep within the earth or deeper yet within the black silent tombs of Polish memory. But this is not the case across the road.

Opposite the monument is a small stand of trees set back a few yards from the road. Ramatowski leads us down a small ditch littered with trash—empty bottles, a mangled high chair, empty baby-food jars, rotting diapers—and up into the woods. Here, he explains, is the former Jewish cemetery, which used to extend all the way to the main road. Most of it has since been plowed under for potato crops, but the trees that stand here have spared this particular corner of the centuries-old cemetery from the plowshare. We enter the dense woods, crashing our way through tangles of barren underbrush. The earth has given way in places to the collapsed coffins beneath, creating slight indentations as gentle and subtle as a sigh. In other places, deep, marked incisions in the earth suggest that graves have been plundered. Everywhere there are toppled jagged stones, some half buried. Were it not for the worn Hebrew inscriptions, one might mistake them for natural rock outcroppings. As we march through the woods, pausing silently to stare into a plundered grave or study an inscription, our footsteps break the silence, crushing dried leaves and snapping twigs. I stumble repeatedly over thick broken branches—their bark has been stripped away and pale surface bleached white by the elements—scattered among the fallen brown foliage. Only when I look more closely do I see that they are human bones. Dozens of them. Large, thick leg bones, and the thinner bones of forearms. Some have been shattered, revealing the porous structure beneath, but most lie whole and scattered among the leaves. It is here that I finally come across the first concrete traces of the Jewish community of Jedwabne. Here they lie, just beyond the rotting diapers and debris of Polish life, forgotten and protected. Somewhere here in this woods are the bones—the charred flesh long since gone—of Michael Kuropatve the wagondriver, who did not want a life given to him by murderers, and the old Rabbi Bialystocky and the thousand other Jews whose screams and burning flesh filled the fields and wafted over the rooftops of the neighboring houses, and, most important for my purposes, the bones of the stern Jewish grain merchant and his lovely, forgiving wife, Abraham and Lenta Zaidenstadt.

When we reemerge from the woods, dusk is falling. As I step from the ditch back onto the road, I lose my breath for an instant, and the world tumbles around me, and around the racing furrows of the fields, the somber houses of the village, and the twin white towers of the Jedwabne Cathedral rising victoriously in the falling night sky. Up the road, an elderly Polish farmer is driving a small clutch of cows from his fields back to town. The cows bolt and jostle along the rutted road. The farmer is ancient, his face creased and deeply tanned with age. It would seem he has been walking this same stretch of road for centuries. As he approaches us, I ask my father to see if the farmer recalls anything about the barn or the Jews. When my father stops him to ask if he knows anything about the Jews who died here, the man replies, "Jakie Zydzi?"—What Jews?—and presses on.

23

WE ARE IN LUCK. We have arrived in Poland in time for Armistice Day, when Europe commemorates the fallen soldiers of the First World War, and the veterans of the 33rd Regiment have gathered in Łomza. We are given this intelligence by the doorman at our hotel, who himself was in the 33rd, and though he never knew Mjetek Zaideta, he does know Colonel Ziłowski, the head of the 33rd's veteran association. We can meet Ziłowski, he tells us, if we show up at the Łomza Cathedral the following morning for the ten o'clock mass, when the bishop will bless the colonel, the veterans, and the color standards of the 33rd. The colonel, he says, will be a uniformed man with the largest white mustache we have ever seen.

When we arrive the following morning, the cathedral square is teeming with every man, woman, and child in Łomza, even the beggars. Everyone is wrapped in thick coats and warm hats against the bitter, clear-sky cold, except for a cluster of Gypsy children who sit bareheaded with open palms at the cathedral entrance. A uniformed brass ensemble, gleaming brilliantly in the morning light, leads a column of bemedaled veterans into the square, plumes of vapor pouring forth from their greatcoated ranks. The column marches into the cathedral, where it then dissolves, spilling into the pews and lining the main aisle with a double column of red and white banners emblazoned with a stylized Polish eagle. These are the men of the 33rd Łomza, the unwavering ranks that for two bitter weeks back in 1939 held their ground along the Narva River while the rest of the Polish army reeled under the German advance.

For the next two hours, we watch the bishop of Łomza, whose satin-robed predecessor once peddled the coinage of false security to the twelve hundred Jews of Jedwabne, as he bestows his blessings on the parish, on the soldiers, then marches up and down the aisle showering the double row of eagle-spangled banners with holy water. The cathedral resounds with the chanting of the Our Father, the Hail Mary, and the Apostles' Creed, followed by a rousing chorus, "Long Live Poland."

Afterward, at the monument to the 33rd Łomza Regiment, three salvos of a twenty-one-gun salute crack in the crisp air, sending birds into the bitterly cold blue sky. Another invocation of "Long Live Poland," then a procession to the local movie theater, which on this day provides a stage for a folk-dance extravaganza. After two hours of vigorous boot stomping and gold-brocade-skirt twirling, which occasionally permits glimpses of the upper thighs of Łomza's dozen or so most beautiful girls, the event concludes with a final rendering of "Long Live Poland."

In the course of the five-hour sojourn, my father moves from one khaki-green greatcoat to the next, invoking the name Mjetek Zaideta. He is told numerous stories of heroism against overwhelming odds—the 33rd Łomza shattered the Brandenburg Division along the Narva, whose water ran red with German blood— and views countless battle wounds. One veteran pulls up his shirt to display a stomach wound; another removes his fur hat and runs his hand over a bald pate that is patchworked with shrapnel scars. "Our commanding officer gave us orders not to surrender," one veteran explains. "After that he was killed and our lines of communication were cut. Our last order was not to surrender, so we didn't." The veterans remember the shriek of the Stuka bombers, the roar of the German 88s, and the smell of diesel-driven Panzers as vividly as if it were yesterday, but no one here remembers Mjetek Zaideta, the Jewish recruit from Jedwabne who was spared the gas chambers by the friendship of his Polish comrades-in-arms. "I knew a Jew named Orłowski, a good, decent man," one officer tells me. "He came from a well-to-do family and studied at the university in France. We all knew Orłowski was a Jew, but no one ever betrayed him. We stuck together. The Germans were our common enemy."

Unfortunately, Colonel Ziłowski does not recall Infantryman Zaideta either. With the white tips of his mustache rising and falling like bird wings, the colonel recounts his own failed attempts to locate missing comrades, blames the Germans for destroying many of the records and the Russians for confiscating the rest. As far as he knows, there is no complete record of the 33rd Łomza's three thousand officers and enlisted men. He notes, however, that fragments of records do exist, and recommends that we check the local archive in down-town Łomza.

The next morning, we visit the Łomza City Archive, a small concrete building behind a handsome brick schoolhouse that served as Gestapo headquarters during the German occupation. While the director and I lament the dearth of archival material—he has nothing on Jedwabne nor the 33rd Lomza—my father, hat on head and coat on rack, chatters away with the receptionist. Before long, she is on the telephone.

Half an hour later, we are sitting in the office of Andrzej Piłoski, the curator of the Łomza Museum. Situated on the third floor of an old villa filled with displays—including four examples of the famous spinning wheels produced by Jedwabne craftsmen—Piłoski's office is cluttered with books, papers, and assorted documents. On one wall is a large German-language map of Europe dating from 1944. Except for the bloated proportions of the Reich and the reduced dimensions of the Polish territory, the European borders do not look much different from those of Europe today. Czechoslovakia is divided into the two separate nations. The Balkans are a pastiche of fragmented nations; a notation at the bottom of the map reads: "The borders of the former Yugoslavia remain in dispute." Some things never change.

A stern man in his mid-forties who dresses in academic tweeds, Curator Piłoski tells us that there is virtually no written information on the 33rd Łomza, that the Russians destroyed or confiscated virtually all documentation, and that there are no complete enlistment rolls.

He then walks across the room and produces three thick files, one of which contains the memoirs of the commander of the 33rd Łomza, dictated in 1992, shortly before his death, and transcribed onto 120 typewritten pages; and another containing diverse newspaper articles on the 33rd; and a third containing an extensive but incomplete list of 33rd Łomza officers and infantrymen. For the next half-hour, we sit across from Piłoski as he runs his finger down column after column of names, which seem to be organized in no particular order. Nowotny beside Aranski and Zelinski and Baronszic and Feldmann and Grobowski. But, as it turns out, no Mjetek Zaideta.

24

Y ALE R EISNER REACHES into a box, removes a large sheaf of paper, and begins flipping through the pages. After a moment, he pauses, looks up at me.

"What did you say his name was?"

"Zaidenstadt."

"And the town again?"

"Jedwabne."

Sitting in a third-floor office of the Jewish Historical Institute in Warsaw, I watch as Reisner flips through a six-inch stack of photocopied pages. As director of research and archives of the Ronald S. Lauder foundation, Reisner has spent the last three years linking Jews with their roots in Poland. Scattered about the cramped office are the tools of Reisner's trade, reference works in Hebrew, Yiddish, Polish, and English, piles of photocopied documents, and an outdated Apple computer. A hundred or so blue passports dating from the 1930s, stamped with transit visa from Poland through Romania to Palestine, lie heaped on a table. On one wall a yellowed poster from the 1940s advertises Hans Brandmark, a German liqueur produced in Oswiecim, Poland, home to the Auschwitz extermination camp.

"Was his father a grain merchant?" Reisner asks matter-of-factly.

I look at him in amazement. "In fact, he was."

"Was his name Abraham or Chone?"

"Abraham."

"Here is your man," Reisner says, handing me a photocopied page from the 1929 *Księga Adresowa Polski*, the national business directory. The entry for Jedwabne, on page 127, notes that the town has a population of 1,428, that the nearest rail connection is fourteen kilometers away in Łomza, that it has a cathedral, a brick factory, a windmill, and a market that is open every Monday. There follows a full column of fifty names or so, and beside each one the particular service they offer, butchers, barbers, bakers, blacksmiths, druggists, a wagon builder, and toward the end of the column, an entry *Żboze*—grains—with three names: Goldberg Ch., Zajdensztadt A., and Zajdensztat Ch. The first documented evidence of the Zaidenstadt family.

When I express astonishment that he achieved in less than five minutes what has eluded me for the past five months, Yale dismisses the praise, saying that is his job, trying to reconstruct extinguished lives, seeking to connect sons and daughters to their deceased parents. In most cases, he finds himself simply seeking eyewitness testimony or written proof to confirm that a particular person had indeed died. "I recently was able to provide a woman with a death certificate for her sister who had died of typhus in the Warsaw Ghetto," he says. "It was sad news, but at least the sister had a date and a reason for her sister's death. It helped bring closure." Yale cites another case in which he brought together a mother and son each of whom had assumed the other was long dead.

"On the one hand it was wonderful to bring them together," Yale says. "On the other, they realized they had missed a lifetime together." He says he receives a hundred "walk-ins"—like me—each month, and literally thousands of written requests. "As you can imagine, there is quite a backlog."

Yale is intrigued by my interest in Jedwabne, noting that this tiny village has been making news in Latin America in the last few weeks. "A Jewish man named Wasserstein has been claiming that the Poles burned Jews during the German occupation," Yale says. "The Polish ambassador has written to the Polish Foreign Ministry asking for clarification, and the ministry has turned to us for clarification." Yale says there are only two documented cases in which Poles literally burned Jews alive, one in Bialystok, a large town seventy kilometers east of Łomza, where the Poles packed the local synagogue with its Jewish worshipers and set it ablaze. And, of course, the barn burning in Jedwabne. "It was not a common practice," Yale tells me, "but it did happen."

Yale then returns to the matter at hand, the Zaidenstadt family. Though he is pressed for time, Yale insists that he should be able to find more significant documentation, possibly a birth certificate, a property deed, a business transaction. He checks several reference works in his office, including *Jewish Roots in Poland*. Next he types "Jedwabne" and "Zaidenstadt" into his computer. When all these searches bring nothing, he disappears down the hall to check the institute's archive. He returns fifteen minutes later empty-handed. According to the records he has consulted, there are no birth certificates, no business records, and no death certificates for any of the Jedwabne Jews. "From the looks of it," Yale muses, "they burned more than the barn."

25

IN THE SPRING OF 1941, just months before the Jews of Jedwabne fell prey to the bloody thirsts of their Polish neighbors, Johanna Hirschberger received a letter from her brother Michael, stating his intent to close accounts with America. "My dearest Johanna," the letter began, "I am writing to tell you that I have made the decision to come home. After the past year, it is clear to me that things cannot go on like this. At first I had thought that I could manage without Midge, but it is now clear to me that this is simply not possible. I considered moving to Milwaukee to be closer to Frank and Elisabeth, but after speaking with them, I know this would never work; they insist on legal guardianship over Gail and Marge, which is something I can never agree to. And so, here I sit. A forty-eight-year-old widower with a pile of debt, two teenage girls to raise, and no one to help."

By the spring of 1941 it seemed indeed as if my grandfather had played out his hand in America. Following his tour of Europe, he had sought to capitalize on the end of prohibition. Securing the first liquor license in Sauk Centre, he opened Werner's Liquors in a vacant store next to the First State Bank on the corner of Main and Fourth streets. When community leaders forced him to close the store because of its proximity to the Sauk Centre High School, my grandfather plunged headlong into a series of business disasters—a grocery store in Glenwood, a bottling plant for a non-carbonated soda called Cold Spot, a Minneapolis-based cosmetic line, named after my mother, called Patsy Gaye—that gradually sapped his financial and emotional resources. His final venture, a nightclub called Hoboken House, a mile and half outside Sauk Centre, comple-mented his gregarious nature but also fed his two great-est vices—drinking and gambling.

One evening following a card game in which he lost almost fifty dollars, my grandfather decided he had had enough for one night. Throwing back a final drink, he took Midge to his car, a 1939 hard-top Pontiac, and roared down Hoboken Hill toward Sauk Centre. It was a bitter cold night with a punishing wind that whipped snow squalls across the road. At the railway crossing just outside of town, a freight train flashed through the blinding snow. He slammed on the brakes but the car skidded on ice. Hurtling headlong into the side of a passing boxcar, the Pontiac was dragged along the tracks for nearly fifty feet before it broke free and plummeted down the embankment. My grandmother was killed instantly; my grandfather sustained a brain concussion and multiple internal injuries.

When my grandfather was finally released from the hospital, and found himself confronting life without his wife, he set about simplifying matters as best he could. With his son already gainfully employed in Detroit as a tool and dye maker, he dispatched his two daughters, ages eleven and thirteen, to Catholic boarding schools in Little Falls, an hour and a half's drive from Sauk Centre. Left on his own, however, he quickly dissipated. Riven by guilt and grief, he suffered extended periods of despondency and turned increasingly to alcohol. When he wasn't at the Hoboken House "overseeing things," he was playing cards at local pubs in downtown Sauk Centre, or sitting alone at home with a cigar, in every case with a drink in hand. As his attentiveness to business lapsed, his financial interests faltered; soon he was selling off properties to make ends meet. The country that had given him everything—love, success, a family—a quarter-century earlier was gradually taking it all back. By the spring of 1941, Mike Werner found himself alone, a foreigner in a foreign land.

It was in this moment of cruel abandonment that my grandfather picked up a pen in the spring of 1941 and wrote to his sister Johanna that the time had come for him to return home. "I came home that Easter from boarding school," my mother recalls. "He had had a lot to drink and was in an excited state, and kept pacing up and down in the living room with a cigar in his hand, and saying that he had come up with an idea that would solve all our problems." According to my mother, he then launched into a vivid evocation of the gentle Gail Valley with its rising peaks, reminding my mother that it was this very valley that had given her her name. "He then told me of his intentions to take me and my sister to Förolach with him," my mother says. "He said he wanted to talk with the nuns in Little Falls about teaching us German." That afternoon, when a neighbor stopped by for a drink, my grandfather started boasting about his large house in Förolach and the tracts of farm-land that he, as the eldest son, had inherited. When my grandfather outlined his plans to return "home" to Europe, the neighbor stared at him in disbelief and laughed. "Mike, are you crazy? There's a war going on over there." "Not for long," my grandfather replied, tapping his cigar on the edge of his ashtray. "Not for long."

By the spring of 1941, to many Germans, the war seemed to be virtually over. The jackbooted armies of the Reich had crushed resistance in Poland, France, Scandinavia, and the Lowlands; Hitler had secured a nonaggression pact with Russia; and America wanted no part of this most recent European bloodbath. Rommel was in North Africa pummeling the Reich's zone of safety to the very borders of Egypt. Hitler still had the annoying business of bombing the British into submission, but with the continent firmly in hand, with Germany flush with victory and awash in the spoils of war, and with Austria safely tucked into the southern comfort of the Reich, there seemed little reason for my grand-father not to return home.

Migration records indicate that my grandfather was not alone in his deliberations. Following the Nazi seizure of power in 1933 and the ensuing stabilization of the German economy, several hundred thousand natu-ralized Americans of German and Austrian descent, many of whom had fled the political and economic chaos of the Weimar Republic, packed their bags and headed home. Though contemporary demographers re-fer to this migratory anomaly as "reflux migration," for the Germans of the day this phenomenon paraded brassily under the banner of *Heim ins Reich*—back home to the Reich.

My mother spent most of Easter Saturday riding her horse in the fields around Hoboken Hill. The following day, the family went to Sunday mass, then to have Easter dinner with a friend in the nearby town of Morris. On the drive back home, my grandfather stopped to help a man push his vehicle from a snowbank, and that night, as a result of the strain, suffered a massive heart attack. Hearing his groans of agony, my mother bolted from her bed and ran into his room to find him clutching his chest and calling weakly for Midge. By the time the family doctor arrived a half an hour later, Mike Werner was dead.

It is hard to say whether my grandfather would have ever seriously undertaken the move to Förolach, or whether his plans were simply a passing whimsy fueled by grief and too much drink, or whether, if indeed he had been serious, the Japanese attack on Pearl Harbor that December, and America's subsequent declaration of war against both Germany and Japan, would have idled his plans. A coronary thrombosis on the night of April 14, 1941, made all this speculation moot. Nevertheless, I cannot help but express quiet awe that, at least for a brief few days in the spring of 1941, a thirteen-year-old girl growing up in heartland America was quite literally a heartbeat away from a life in Nazi Germany.

26

"When i die, I'd like to be cremated in that oven," Martin says to me, pointing to the large brick oven on the far right of the crematorium room. Of the four large ovens in the room, it is the only one that still appears to be fully operational. Not only can the doors be locked, but the large metal tray on which the body is slid into the oven chamber can still be run along the tracks into the oven interior. Martin looks at me, waiting to gauge my reaction to this notion. He smiles, obviously entertained by the horror of it.

It is pouring outside. The gray overcast skies have ripped open and delivered a violent torrent that hammers on the roof and sends the gravel leaping into the air with each hurtling drop of rain. The visitors initially scramble for cover in the crematorium and gas chamber, but as the storm continues with unrelenting intensity, gradually, one by one then in small groups, they set out from Baracke X, their heads bowed against the storm, or their umbrellas sagging under the deluge. At the moment, we are alone in the crematorium room with its four ovens, their iron-jawed maws empty and cold. The brick chimney rises to the A-frame ceiling, the heavy crossbeams lending the room a hint of ski-lodge ambiance. In the humid air, the musty smell of ash rises from the ovens.

Martin reaches into his satchel, takes out a packet of crackers; he offers me one, then takes one for himself. He chews slowly and deliberately. I have never seen him consume any liquid nor make use of the restroom behind the crematorium. With his leathery skin, and his dry wit, he seems to possess a crusty tortoise-like resilience that has transcended aging, a static state of *being* old, not *growing* old. You can imagine Martin being like this forever. Propped on his cane, only occasionally does he shift his weight from one leg to the other.

Martin is in a good mood today. He has been telling me about his childhood in Poland again, in particular about his mother and her beautiful voice. Occasionally, he breaks into a children's song, or a Hebrew chant, then pauses as if to watch it melt in the air and smiles at the memory.

When the rain eventually subsides, Martin goes outside, and fifteen minutes later the first visitors come walking into the compound. As a young man wearing a Dave Matthews Band T-shirt, with a Discman and mirrored sunglasses—despite the overcast skies—saunters across the bridge, Martin fixes his sights on him and moves in. "American?"

The young man slips the earphone to the side, and lets the sunglasses slide off his nose and swing down below his chin, the frames clinging miraculously to his ears. "Come again?"

"American?" Martin repeats.

"No, man, Australian."

"Australia?" Martin says with surprise. He studies the young man for a moment, then looks down at his own jacket, and runs his finger down his lapel, saying, "Pins, pins, pins, pins." Pins . . . stripes . . . pinstripes— I assume Martin is trying to describe the stripes of the concentration camp uniform. But the Aussie, his mirrored sunglasses bobbing beneath his clean-shaved chin, knows exactly what the old man is trying to tell him.

"Yeah, man—pins," he laughs.

Martin smiles, and gleefully sings, "Pins, pins, pins, pins, pins," again running his hand down his jacket.

"Kangaroos," the Aussie says.

"And maple leaf," Martin adds. "Leaf, leaf, leaf, leaf," again running his finger down his lapel. "Canada and Australia," Martin says with a big smile. "Pins, pins, pins, pins, pins."

"You from here?"

"Three and half years in camp," Martin says. "I come every day for fifty years. Barbara Distel says gas chamber never used. But I hear screams. I have photographs. Barbara Distel only two years old when I here. I know. Gas chamber here. Ovens here. Mosquito barracks over there. General Rommel in Africa. Prisoners have mosquitoes on them. For General Rommel in Africa. You don't understand?"

"Wow, like you survived this place," comes the response. "Like you're a real Holocaust survivor." He shakes his head with astonishment, flips his glasses back onto his nose, slides his earphones back into place, and marches off toward the gas chamber. Martin stands smiling. "Pins, pins, pins, pins," Martin murmurs. "Two boxes at home. Maple leaves and kangaroos."

At one point, three people enter the compound: a short, elderly man in a Ralph Lauren polo shirt with a completely bald head; his diminutive wife, barely four and a half feet, if that, with jet-black hair; and their son, who appears to be in his late twenties, a cross between a football halfback and a bouncer at a college-town bar. Martin approaches them and begins to speak English, but the man answers in German. He was born in Frankfurt and arrested by the Nazis in 1942 and sent to a sub-camp of Sachsenhausen outside Berlin. He went to the States after the war, and set up a dry-cleaning business in Chicago. He is in Europe now for the first time since then. He wanted to show his son his former camp near Sachsenhausen; he also wanted to bring him to Dachau, to show him where his two uncles died. When he finishes speaking, Martin tells him that his name is Martin Zaidenstadt, that he survived the camp, that he has been coming here every day for the past fifty years.

"Maybe you knew my uncles?" the man replies.

"There were many people in Dachau."

"Kurt Moses and Albert Moses. Both died here. Maybe you knew them?"

"No, I did not know them. There were many people here. Where did they come from?"

"Frankfurt. The entire family from Frankfurt. Me too."

"Frankfurt," Martin says. "So a German Jew."

"Yes."

"Where were you born? In Germany?" Martin asks.

"In Frankfurt."

"In Frankfurt?"

"And I was in a camp in Berlin. I just told you that."

"In Berlin?"

"In Berlin."

"There was a camp in Berlin?"

"Oh, yes, Sachsenhausen."

"It was a prison, not a camp."

The man looks at Martin in astonishment and laughs out loud. "Go there and see for yourself. Sachsenhausen was a concentration camp. It's still there."

"But only afterward," Martin replies. "They built it afterward. It was only a camp afterward."

"But it was still a camp."

"The first camp was here in Dachau."

"I didn't say that Sachsenhausen was the first camp. I only said it was a camp."

"Sachsenhausen, Mauthausen, Neuengamme, Natzweiler, Auschwitz, Maidanek, Theresienstadt, Treblinka, Bergen-Belsen, Sobibor," Martin starts to chant, then pauses and adds. "But at Sobibor they had the children. That's where they gassed the children."

"No," the man retorts, "they gassed the children at Treblinka."

"I said it was Sobibor."

The two survivors banter back and forth in German like two Americans arguing about which baseball team traded which pitcher during which season. They cannot agree on anything, on which camps had gas chambers and which did not, on which camps performed medical experiments, about which camp was the largest, the harshest, the worst, or the first. Throughout, Martin keeps repeating that Dachau was the first camp, until the man finally throws his hands in the air. "I know that Dachau and Buchenwald were the first camps! You don't have to keep telling me."

"What are you talking about!" Martin yells at him. "Buchenwald was not the first camp. Dachau was the first camp, and I was here for two and a half years." The man stares at Martin. A stillness descends between the two men, and when they speak again, their tone is subdued.

"In which year?" the man asks, starting anew.

"In thirty-three," Martin replies.

"No, what year were you here?"

"The first camp was Dachau," Martin repeats.

"I already told you, I *know* that."

"No, you said the other camp."

"Which other camp?"

"Buchenwald, you said Buchenwald was the first camp."

"It is a fact," the man says. "Buchenwald and Dachau were the first camps. It was only later that they built Auschwitz and the other camps."

"I already said that," Martin retorts, and begins again: "Bergen-Belsen, Mauthausen, Neuengamme, Natzweiler, Treblinka, Maidanek, Sobibor, Auschwitz . . ."

"And where do you live now?" he interrupts Martin.

"Here in Dachau."

"No, no, I mean where do you live now?"

"I told you, here in Dachau."

"You live here, in the camp?"

Martin grins. "In Dachau," he says. "There is a city called Dachau."

"Oh, oh, oh, I understand, in the city, not in the camp," the survivor says. "I went to America. I am an American now."

"Where do you live in America?"

"In Chicago."

"Chicago? Al Caponi," Martin says and makes the sound of a machine gun. They both laugh.

"You work here in Dachau? You have a business?

"I don't work."

"So, you live from compensation."

"I never received anything."

"I also got nothing," the survivor replies. "Nothing at all."

"I was here in Dachau. Two and a half years and I don't receive a single pfennig."

The two men begin to rail against the German government and how the Germans refuse to pay them compensation, and against the Jewish community in Germany and how they have forgotten about Jews like Martin, and then Martin starts to talk about a New York rabbi with red hair who did not believe Martin was a Jew until Martin recited the Kaddish for him, at which point Martin begins to chant, and is then joined by his fellow survivor. As they sing they look into each other's eyes, like two long-lost drinking buddies, and when they finish, Martin asks, "How old are you?"

"How old? I am seventy."

"How old am I?" Martin asks.

"What?"

"How old am I?"

"I don't know, eighty? Eighty-three?"

"Eighty-seven!" Martin says as if it is a triumph.

"They took me when I was just a boy," the survivor suddenly says. "First they took my father, then my uncles, my aunts, my grandparents. One day they called. They told my mother to come to them. She went to the head of the SS, to his office, and she never came back. Then I was there all alone with my five sisters. Six children, all alone. The next morning they took my big sister away, to Theresienstadt. They sent me and my other four sisters to Berlin. We were in a detainment camp. Actually it was a Jewish hospital, but during the war it was used as a detainment camp. They would wait until it was full of Jews and then they would send them all to Auschwitz. I was sent to a work camp. Sachsenhausen was already full, so they sent our truck to Wolheide. I was there for three years. I worked there until the Russians came and liberated us." He pauses, looks at Martin, then glances slowly about the camp. "My uncles, Kurt Moses, Sauli Moses, Albert Moses, they were all here in Dachau."

"How long were they here?" Martin asks.

"They sent them here in 1938, and after a couple of months they let them go and sent them all back home, and then they were sent back here and then it was all over."

"Here in Dachau?"

"My uncle Albert and my aunts went to Auschwitz,"

he says, then corrects himself. "No, it wasn't Auschwitz, it was . . ."

"Maidanek?" Martin asks.

"No, no, not Maidanek."

"Treblinka, Mauthausen, Neuengamme, Natzweiler," Martin begins to recite but his fellow survivor cuts him off. "No, no, no, with the ship to Shanghai."

"Shanghai?" Martin says with surprise. "Shanghai was not a concentration camp."

"In 1939, they took the last ship to Shanghai," he says. "Then, after the war they went to America."

"Shanghai? Do you speak Chinese?" Martin asks, and before waiting for a reply begins speaking words I cannot understand but which have the rising and falling inflection of an East Asian language. Martin stops after a moment and smiles. I cannot tell whether he is pulling our leg or not.

"I wasn't in Shanghai," the man says. "I was in Wolheide. The Russians liberated me."

"Gavaryu pa russki?" Martin asks.

"Da."

Martin intones a Russian song, a somber melody with thick words written for deep voices and a hard life, and as he sings, his fellow survivor joins in. The two men sing until they lose the words and the melody trails off. "Anyhow," the man says, "that's my life."

"You want to take a picture of me?" Martin suddenly asks.

While the son unpacks his camera, the two men walk over to the statue on its stone pedestal. The camera flashes three times, and the ritual return of these brothers of the concentration camp fraternity ends. "You send me a copy?" Martin asks.

"Sure," the man replies. "What is your address?"

Martin reaches into his pocket and removes his stack of cards, and as he is handing one to the man, he mutters, "These cards are expensive, you know."

The man stares at him, and says in a knowing voice, "How much?"

Martin shrugs his shoulders and repeats, "These cards are expensive."

"George!" His wife hisses as he reaches into his pocket for his billfold. Ignoring her, he removes a twenty-dollar bill and without a word presses it into Martin's hand, then turns and walks away with his wife and son. Martin watches them until they reach the bridge, then takes the twenty-dollar bill, studies it for a moment, folds it in half, and presses it deep into his pocket.

27

MARTIN RUNS HIS FINGER ALONG the gash in his desktop and lets me know in no uncertain terms that he has no tolerance for those who claim that he is not telling the truth. "A former SS man came to visit me last month," Martin tells me. "He said what I was saying was untrue, that I was spreading lies, that the gas chamber was never used. Who was he to tell me what happened in that camp? I was there. I saw it with my own eyes. I did not need to argue with him, and I told him so. I told him to get out of my house. He refused to leave. He told me he was going to finish the discussion, so I took out my gun and shot at him."

Martin shows me the gash with evident pride. For him, his three-inch-long, finger-thick channel plowed through the thin veneer and pressed-wood surface of his desk by a .380 caliber bullet is adequately compelling evidence that he is a man of his convictions. When Martin says something, he means it.

I follow the trajectory of the bullet from the desk to a hole in the wall near the door, and try to imagine the look of dismay on his visitor's face when Martin reached into his desk drawer, pulled out the pistol, and brought his finger to the trigger. This had the makings of the kind of headlines that Dachauers fear most: a Holocaust survivor, a former SS officer, a loaded pistol, and all of them in a two-story house in a residential neighborhood in Dachau. Fortunately for Dachau—and the survivor and the former Nazi—the story apparently only made it as far the Dachau police station.

According to Martin, the man reported the incident to the police, who came to Martin's house to investigate. "I have a license for my gun," Martin assures me. "I showed it to them, and told them what had happened. They know Martin Zaidenstadt. They know he is a good man. They know he always tells the truth."

On this particular day, I have come to Martin to give him the Yizkor book on Jedwabne and to show him my snapshots of my recent visit to Poland, though I spare him the photographs of the demolished Jewish cemetery with its scattered and broken bones.

When I show Martin the book, he says, "Only this much? I could write three books on Jedwabne." As Martin glances through the photographs, portraits of Itzchok Yenkel and Eliezer Piekarz and the Cinowitz family, he dismisses them. Why does he need photographs? He remembers everyone in town exactly as they were. He immediately recognizes Avigdor Rosenblatt, whose father ran the bakery right next-door to the Zaidenstadt house. One day, Martin recalls, two Polish boys threw a cobblestone through the Rosenblatt window, and Avi, a hot-tempered twelve-year-old, charged from the house brandishing a large knife, intent on killing the two goyim. The slaughter was only averted by Martin, two years Avi's senior, who dashed out to the street and wrested the knife from the would-be killer.

Martin's eyes light up with youthful delight and mischief as he evokes a small town with warm, heated houses, streets bustling with Jews, the smell of bread wafting into the streets, the arrival of the greengrocer with fresh produce from the fields, the Monday market bustling with farmers from the surrounding region. His memory populates the snapshots with Jedwabne's vanished Jews, and suddenly you can see the Blunsteins, and the Kraumüllers and Gunfaron the baker all plying their trades. At moments he breaks into song as he recalls his mother, a lovely woman who had an eye for handsome men and used to appear in the street to chat and flirt; his father, a strict and stern man who was quick with the thick leather strap and serious about keeping the Sabbath, about his disapproval of Martin playing soccer with the Polish boys in town. "Look at you, Motel," he used to say. "You run like a *shaigitz*." One Sabbath on the way to the temple, Martin was waylaid by the Polish boys, and headed off for a game of soccer instead of going to afternoon prayers. When Martin returned home, his father asked him how the prayers had been. "They were just fine, Father," Martin replied.

"And who read the prayers today, Motel?" his father asked.

"Avi Goldstein," Martin responded. But his father knew better, he had heard from a neighbor, and Martin was whacked thrice with the thick leather strap, once for lying to his father, once for playing soccer with the *shaigitzi*, and once for—the worst offense—having missed temple. On another occasion, a neighbor saw Martin go into the shop of the Polish butcher and reported this to Martin's father. When his father asked him if had eaten Polish meat, Martin responded that he had gone in to change money. "Give me your hands, Motel," his father demanded, then lifted them to his nose, and sniffed his son's palms.

Martin's eyes veritably sparkle with warm memories as he recounts his holy misdemeanors, but a tone of affectionate respect descends upon him when he invokes the name of Rabbi Bialystocky, the gentle and pious man with the great beard, who would not work on the Sabbath, not even light his own fire or tear a piece of paper out of respect for the Sabbath, who—according to Martin—advised the Jewish children of Jedwabne not to walk in the woods on the Sabbath because they might step on a stick and break it. Also an act of labor. Recognizing the intelligence, wit, and vaulting independence of the young Mordechai Zaidenstadt, Rabbi Bialystocki once told Martin, "You will grow up to be either a rabbi or a rebel."

Like his father, Martin became a grain dealer. After studying at the Yeshiva in Łomza, and serving his mandatory duty in the Polish army, Martin returned to Jedwabne, moved back in with the family, and entered the family grain business. He learned to keep books, deal with the Polish farmers, and, on occasion, serve as a counterweight for measuring the grain sacks as they were loaded into the wagon and sent to Łomza.

But as good as life seemed, the Jews of Jedwabne lived under the specter of seething Polish hatred. In one famous incident a Polish woodchopper in Jedwabne threatened to kill his Jewish neighbor who had declined his invitation to dine with him. The Jew begged to be allowed to say a prayer before his death, and fell to his knees. Moved by the Jew's piousness, the Pole spared him his life. Prayers were, it seemed, all the Jews of Jedwabne had to protect them from the envy and wrath of the Polish farmers. As early as 1937, Martin's father knew Poland was no place for the Jews, and he began a gradual process of dispersing his children. He sent his daughter Feiga to live in Argentina; his son Yankel, to avoid serving in the Polish military, emigrated to Cuba, and after Castro came to power, moved to Miami where he raised a family. In 1939, shortly before the German invasion, the elder Zaidenstadt sought to move the rest of his family to Palestine, but the British required one thousand pounds sterling as an entrance fee, more money than a Jewish grain merchant in northern Poland could manage in 1939. When a relative living in Jerusalem refused to vouch for the money, Martin's father abandoned the plan. "Because he refused to guarantee the money," Martin says, "I lost my entire family. My mother, my father, my aunt and uncle, my cousins, my sister Malka and her husband Gronski, my niece and my nephew, my wife and daughter. All burned ... All gone." Wife and daughter? This is the first time in our two years of acquaintance that Martin has ever mentioned a wife and daughter in Poland. When I express surprise, he looks muddled for a moment. His mind has careened from one positive association to another, and has suddenly landed him on a dark path he has avoided in all our discussions during the past two years. He hesitates for a moment, then plunges into the abyss of memory. Yes, he had been married before, to Sala Gingraz, a lovely girl from Jedwabne with whom he had fallen in love. When he completed his studies in Łomza, they had married, moved in with Martin's parents, and brought into the world a beautiful baby girl. Martin was as happy as any man could be. In the summer of 1939, as tensions between Germany and Poland made war seem inevitable, Martin was conscripted into the 33rd Łomza Regiment. That August, Sala visited him in Łomza. She left their daughter at home. At the time, it seemed like the right thing to do.

It is here that Martin stumbles. He falls silent. His face hardens into an expression I cannot read. His eyes that can alternately convey such subtle humor or such intense rage, that always engage one with such immediacy, suddenly grow distant, gazing beyond me and the room. The girl's age? The girl's name? He does not say. Instead, he extends his right arm with his palm open, indicating a child the same height as my four-year-old daughter. Martin's outstretched arm hovers motionless, his open palm resting on the memory of his daughter's head. His eyes grow moist, the tears roll onto his face, tracing small rivulets down his cheeks and along the side of his nose. Like tears springing from stone.

28

"Ich bringe Martin zur Gaskammer."

The barrier rises, I put the car into gear and enter the camp, the tires rumbling softly over the gravel. I follow the inside perimeter of the wall that faces the Alte Römer Strasse, the barrack foundations flashing past at regular intervals. It is a bleak January day, the camp is virtually empty, and I am alone in the car. A cutting wind drives thin sheets of snow across the gravel. I am on my way back to Salzburg and have decided to stop by the camp on the off chance of paying a brief visit to Martin. Normally I would park in the adjacent visitors' lot and make the fifteen-minute pilgrimage on foot to the crematorium area; but I am in a rush today and the weather is harsh. I must also confess to some profound, possibly perverse, fascination with the power of that horrific invocation—*"Ich bringe Martin zur Gaskammer"*—that opens the gates to Martin's world.

Ahead of me, I see the Jewish memorial, a grim granite monument with a wide stone ramp that leads you into a tomblike vault where the Jewish visitors, some wrapped in the white-and-blue flag of Israel, others in a tallith, or simply wearing a ski parka, come to chant the Kaddish into the dank space where their words echo before being carried up a stone chute, like hope into the heavens, or, if you wish, like futile prayers sucked up a chimney and scattered like smoke and ash into a godless gray sky. I turn left at the unattended monument and drive by the Catholic memorial with its large brass bell where a man and woman are reading an inscription, then past the Protestant memorial, a simple concrete structure with a slight Corbusier twist. Ahead of me, Baracke X, this red-brick, black-roofed structure surrounded by the dense stand of evergreens, possesses a fairy-tale charm, like the gingerbread house from Hansel and Gretel.

As I drive toward the bridge that leads into the compound, I see a lone figure. It is Martin, of course, his hat pulled low over his ears, leaning forward heavily on his cane. His presence lends the scene an air of painful desolation. I stop the car before the bridge, and sit there for a moment, feeling the car's heater blasting warm air onto my feet as I watch Martin standing in the cold. The two visitors near the bell now walk past my car. They are bundled in parkas and ski gloves. The man is carrying a copy of *Let's Go Europe*. I hear their feet crunch on the gravel as they walk past me and cross the bridge, where they pause for a moment to study the electrified fence and loose weave of barbed-wife entanglements. When they enter the camp, Martin, who until now has stood as still as a statue, lifts his cane and takes two resolute steps in their direction. The brief gesture is enough to attract their attention and signals Martin's intention to speak with them. They confer for a moment, then walk in his direction. Then the same ritual that has played itself out a thousand times, ten thousand times, echoes in my mind. I mouth to myself the scene I see but cannot hear.

From?

The man and woman look at each other.

Deutsch? English? Polski? Español?
Excuse me?
American?
Yes.

And then follows the routine.

My name is Martin Zaidenstadt.
I survive this camp.
I come here every day for fifty-three years.

Martin gestures to the left and then to the right. You need to enter by the far entrance. The sign in the gas chamber is a lie. The gas chamber was used. I knew the men who closed the doors. I heard the screams as the gas came in. I still do. The man and woman glance at one another, then again at Martin. Martin reaches into his pocket and withdraws his stack of cards. The man leans forward for a closer look. Martin reaches into his pocket again and this time unfolds the tattered article from the *New York Times*. It flaps in the wind. He holds it for them to see but will not let the man take it into his own hands. The man reads a bit of it, then exchanges further words with Martin. After a moment, he reaches into his pocket and takes out a billfold, removes a bill, and presses it into Martin's hand. Martin holds out a card. The man shakes his head and waves the card away. The couple then walk away, leaving Martin alone in the center of the compound.

According to the digital clock above my rearview mirror, it is nearly four o'clock in the afternoon, almost time for Martin to go home. I consider driving across the bridge and offering him a ride, but then think better of it. Standing in this punishing winter wind that blasts through the gas chamber doors and into the vents and flues of the gaping crematory ovens, Martin is at peace. He prefers these common and clichéd horrors of the Holocaust, those he has seen with his own eyes, heard with his own ears, those he shares with a million other survivors, those he has read of in books and seen in films, to the personal horrors of his wife and daughter, horrors he can only imagine. These eyes that have begun to fail him here in Dachau, these ears that no longer accept the sounds around him. In Dachau, Martin has seen and heard the worst of horrors that man ever committed against man, but they are nothing compared to his inner vision of the flaming barn that lit Jedwabne's night-time sky and cast its dancing flames against the rising twin-spired church.

Martin comes to the gas chamber, to this place of palpable horror, to escape the horrors he never knew, the screams he never heard but that have called to him every silent day, every silent hour of his long life, the cries of a wife he once loved, and possibly still does, the screams of a daughter whose age he cannot speak, whose name he cannot utter, whom, out of sheer horror for what she must have suffered, he can only describe with an extended arm and an open palm.

At the age of eighty-seven, Martin feels the biting wind on his cheeks, the chill in his legs, the numbness in his fingers, and the gnawing hunger in his stomach, and knows he is alive. He has survived another day in Dachau. He can slam the gas chamber door at will, he can run the body trays in and out of the crematory ovens a hundred times if he wishes, and no one, not Max Mannheimer, not Barbara Distel, not the voices that call him on the phone or in his dreams, can touch Martin Zaidenstadt here. This is Martin's domain.

Ich bringe Martin zur Gaskammer. He revels in these words, in the fact that they can be repeated day after day. He has survived the gas chamber today as he did fifty years ago, as he has done for the past four years, as he has done, so he believes, for the last half-century. The watchtowers are vacant, the electrified fences idle, the gas ovens cold, and Martin stands triumphant in Dachau. It is the story of death and rebirth, reenacted day in and day out within this walled compound. *Ich bringe Martin zur Gaskammer.* Once again, Martin has entered the gas chambers and come out alive.

Acknowledgments

There are numerous Dachau residents who have helped me during the eight years I have been visiting this town. I appreciate the time taken both by those who helped and encouraged me, and by those who considered me an intruder and a nuisance. Each in his or her own way has contributed to this book, and helped me through the moral and historical complexities of this remarkable place. Sincere gratitude to Barbara Distel, Bruno Schachtner, and Thomas Soyer for all their support and guidance. Further, I would like to acknowledge Richard M. Hunt, under whose tutelage at Harvard University I first explored the moral dilemmas of the postwar German experience. The inquiry and debate he nurtured among his teaching assistants continue into these days. Appreciation also to my many supportive colleagues at the Salzburg Seminar, especially Olin Robison and Amy Hastings, who have created a work environment that has allowed me to continue to grow professionally and intellectually. Heartfelt gratitude, of course, to my agent, Gail Hochman, and my editor, Dan Frank, and his staff whose patience with me, to my continual bewilderment, seems to know no bounds.

Special thanks to Frank Taylor of the W. K. Kellogg Foundation, who, during a walk around the lake at

Schloss Leopoldskron, helped me overcome my initial confusion with this book. When I expressed frustration at not knowing whether to condemn or defend Dachau, he stopped me dead in my tracks with a pointed reprimand: "How arrogant of you! Who do you think you are that you should pass judgment on the people of this town?" On his advice, I have simply let the Dachauers tell their stories, and left the reader to draw his or her own conclusions.

Finally, thanks to my family. To my father, my intrepid interpreter, who has joined me on several reporting sorties into Eastern Europe; to my mother, who generously shared a dark chapter of our family history with me; to my children, Katrina, Brendan, and Audrey, who have helped me see Dachau from fresh perspectives; and most importantly to my wife and good friend, Marie-Louise. This book, like almost everything else I value in life, would not have been possible without her.